Help Me, Information

Help Me, Information

POEMS

David Kirby

Louisiana State University Press
Baton Rouge

Published by Louisiana State University Press
www.lsupress.org

Manufactured in the United States of America
First printing

Designer: Barbara Neely Bourgoyne
Typeface: Sentinel
Printer and binder: Sheridan Books

Jacket/cover photograph: unsplash.com/Greyson Joralemon

Library of Congress Cataloging-in-Publication Data
Names: Kirby, David, 1944– author.
Title: Help me, information : poems / David Kirby.
Description: Baton Rouge : Louisiana State University Press, [2021]
Identifiers: LCCN 2020052697 (print) | LCCN 2020052698 (ebook) | ISBN 978-0-8071-7594-1 (cloth) | ISBN 978-0-8071-7564-4 (paperback) | ISBN 978-0-8071-7601-6 (pdf) | ISBN 978-0-8071-7602-3 (epub)
Subjects: LCGFT: Poetry.
Classification: LCC PS3561.I66 H45 2021 (print) | LCC PS3561.I66 (ebook) | DDC 811/.54—dc23
LC record available at https://lccn.loc.gov/2020052697
LC ebook record available at https://lccn.loc.gov/2020052698

Long distance information, give me Memphis, Tennessee
Help me find the party trying to get in touch with me.

—Chuck Berry

CONTENTS

ACKNOWLEDGMENTS

Thanks to the editors of the following publications for accepting these poems in the first place, occasionally in different versions or with somewhat different titles, and for permission to reprint them here: *The Account:* “The Locomotion”; *American Journal of Poetry:* “Waffle House Index”; *American Poetry Review:* “Foreign Movies,” “Good Seats,” and “The Whys”; *Asheville Poetry Review:* “Bernstein’s Pizza Pagoda”; *Bennington Review:* “The 1909 Air Show at Brescia” and “Don’t Look”; *Birmingham Poetry Review:* “Hitchhike” and “Radioisotope Thermoelectric Generator Ode”; *Diode:* “To My Body”; *Fifth Wednesday Journal:* “Kissing”; *Hollins Critic:* “Sally Go ’Round the Roses”; *Hopkins Journal:* “More Soprano, Please, More Tenor”; *The Hunger:* “I Wish I Were a Cannibal”; *Jung Journal:* “Marie Antoinette” and “Pruno”; *Kenyon Review:* “A Baby in the Piazza”; *Massachusetts Review:* “Then Elvis Dropped to One Knee”; *Missouri Review:* “High School,” “Ode to My Skinny Legs,” “Unspoken,” and “The Woman in the Wall”; *The Nation:* “What the Parrot Said”; *New Ohio Review:* “Europeans Wrapping Knickknacks”; *One:* “Having a Chat with You”; *Paris Review:* “My Girlfriend Killed James Brown”; *Rattle:* “Foreign Movies”; *Shenandoah:* “The Bad Poetry Reading” and “Chasing Jim Taylor”; *Smartish Pace:* “Racing through Pittsburgh with Annie Dillard”; *Southern Review:* “One Good Turn”; *Tampa Review:* “A Momentary Lapse in Judgment”; *Waxwing:* “Man Catches Baby.”

“Legion, for We Are Many” appeared first in my collection *A Temple Gate Called Beautiful* (Farmington, ME: Alice James Books, 2008). “Lewis and Clark Can’t Spell” was included in *Resist Much / Obey Little: Inaugural Poems to the Resistance,* ed. Michael Rothenberg et al. (New York: Spuyten Duyvil, 2017). “This Magic Moment” was featured on the Academy of American Poets’ Poem-a-Day site on November 21, 2014.

Help Me, Information

Radioisotope Thermoelectric Generator Ode

Sure, lots of lousy poems have been written about Adam naming the animals and no doubt lots of lousy scholarship as well, but we're talking about lousy poems here and not lousy scholarship. We'll leave that to the scholars, though not the lousy ones.
And actually there's a bunch of hooey on creationist websites about Adam naming the animals, because there are so many of the little critters that, if Adam had started just a few minutes after Our Creator "breathed the breath of life into his nostrils," as it says in Genesis, he'd still be doing it today, unless he restricted his labor to, not the individual beasts, but to their genera, for each genus contains dozens, even hundreds of species.
So if Adam named each of the known genera only, according to a website I just consulted, "it would have taken him approximately three hours and forty-five minutes to complete the task if we include a five-minute break every hour."
Ha, ha! See? Poets and academics aren't the only idiots in the world.

Here's what we know about names, be they of animals or people or pianos (we'll get to that in a minute) or, from the viewpoint of marketing professor Tim Calkins, businesses. "It's always very tempting to name a company after yourself," says Professor Calkins. "It is simple. It is honest. And for a lot of entrepreneurs, when they're starting a new business, it's the place to start."
Also, it works: Procter & Gamble were people before they became a business, as were the founders of Bose, Duncan Hines, Doc Martens, and the Mayo Clinic, which is named not for the popular sandwich spread but for two brothers, W. W. and Will Mayo.
The Mayo brothers founded their clinic in 1892 along with Augustus Stinchfield, who was smart enough to go with the brothers' name rather than his own.
If your name were Steinway, you could found Steinway & Sons and make and sell high-end pianos.
Or your name could be Steinway and you could have nothing to do with pianos, though "if your name is Joe Steinway," says Professor Calkins, "people

will think you know a lot about classical music and have this association with you that isn't true."

My name is Kirby, and once I was dating this Jewish woman, and when things started to heat up, her father said, "David, I like you, but I wish your name were Greenberg."

"David" means "beloved" in Hebrew—well, not to him.

I'm sure I have a number of the more admirable Jewish character traits and none of the unsavory Aryan ones, such as a fondness for torchlight rallies and the desire to annex parts of the former Czechoslovakia.

Still, I had the wrong name.

Or I was the wrong brand, if you want to put it that way.

In business, the right name can give a company a story, and that's what a company needs to get its brand across, says David Aaker, vice chairman of Prophet, a branding firm.

"Facts don't work," says Mr. Aaker. "People counterargue. They're skeptical. But if you tell them a story, all that goes away."

Duke Ellington's childhood piano teacher had the wonderfully Trollopian name of Marietta Clinkscales. True fact!

Not that she had any choice in the matter, since her mother and father were Mr. and Mrs. Clinkscales and thus relieved of the burden of coming up with a last name.

It's hard enough to come up with a first: a neonatal nurse of my acquaintance tells me it's not atypical for a patient to say something like, "My father is Terrell and my mother is Jennifer, so I want to name my baby Tennifer—how would I spell that?"

Any way you like, she tells them, though before you fill out a birth certificate, you should go out to the parking lot, get in your car, roll the windows up, and scream the baby's name as loudly as you can.

It's not a name, but my new favorite word is spurtle, which is a sort of paddle used to stir soups, stews, broths, and especially porridge, which, considering that the spurtle is Scottish in origin, makes sense, given that a lot more porridge is prepared and consumed in Aberdeen, Glasgow, and Dundee than colcannon, haggis, neeps and tatties, sticky toffee pudding, black pudding, or grouse.

To the job let the tool be suited, be that tool a kitchen utensil or something else entirely.

I mean, you could stir your porridge with a regular spoon or a pencil or a World War II bayonet, for that matter, but wouldn't it taste better if you stirred it with a spurtle?

Verdi's little-known opera *The Battle of Legnano* has everything an opera needs: best friends who are in love with the same woman; a woman who loved one man once but is now totally faithful to the other man, who is her husband; a villainous third man who lusts after the wife; a loyal but weak serving woman who falls into the villain's clutches; a threatening army camped just outside the city gates; and a battle during which one of the best friends dies.

I'm sure you'd like to know which of the friends dies, though I won't say which in case you actually see *The Battle of Legnano,* which you won't because it's almost never staged due to its unpopularity.

There's also a letter slandering the once wavering but now totally steadfast wife, which, like every letter in every opera ever written, swoops in and out of the narrative as it is lost, found, hidden in someone's bosom, and left on some table on which it should not have been left.

Don't read that letter! you want to shout. But they do, and more misery ensues at least until such time as some milquetoasty plot device lifts the mood a little and the curtain comes down.

The Battle of Legnano, though. Who's going to see an opera called *The Battle of Legnano?* Okay, me. But it sounds like a history lesson, not an opera.

The other two thirds of the seats would have been filled on the evening I went if Verdi had called it *Love and Slaughter* or *She Chose the Right One, Alas* or *The Poisoned Letter*—anything but the name he gave it.

The ancient Greeks didn't name their children till they were three because they wanted to make sure they lived.

Maybe we shouldn't name ours till they're twenty-six, since neuroscientists are confirming what car rental companies have already figured out, that the brain doesn't fully mature until age twenty-five.

Till then, the prefrontal cortex, which is the part of the brain that helps curb impulsive behavior, isn't fully developed.

This explains why a colleague of mine says she can teach her students about feminism as long as she doesn't use the word "feminism."

That would alienate a lot of the young men in her classes as well as the young women who think they can gain the respect of such men by agreeing with them, which they can't.

Ever been to Prague? The area in front of the train station is called Sherwood Forest because it's populated by drunks, homeless people, and panhandlers.

I would describe it as seedy rather than dangerous, but why pull the devil by his tail, as the wise people of that city say?

The name is lighthearted and even affectionate, in its way, though something tells me that any monies thieved from the pockets of tourists and passersby become the sole property of the thief and are not scheduled for redistribution to the populace as they might have been in the days of Robin Hood and his merry band.

I do wish my Jewish girlfriend's father had thought better of me.

There's nothing wrong with my name, even if it isn't as grand as that of Good King Wenceslas, who illustrates my point perfectly, since he wasn't.

Sure, he was pious, but he wasn't effective, which is why his brother Boleslaus stabbed him to death.

Boleslaus was also known as Boleslaus the Cruel.

Can you imagine letting your daughter date somebody named Boleslaus the Cruel?

I'd have had a chance if my name had been different.

But if my name had been different, would my life have been different as well?

At the May 4, 1990, memorial service for artist Keith Haring, actor Dennis Hopper referred to him as "my good friend Keith Harington."

That was bad enough by itself. But Hopper then added "and I mean that sincerely," which is what you say when you don't mean it sincerely at all.

Reader, be content with your name.

That said, do what you can to make it soar like a falcon or kestrel.

Let it be the Hope Diamond of names, the Everest, the Cadillac.

Live so that your name becomes a word known to the people of every country, like "okay" and "Coca Cola®."

Let your name be worthy of inclusion on the audio-visual discs aboard the *Voyager* space probes that were launched in 1977 and are now flying through the star systems of our galaxy and are expected to do so until 2025, when their radioisotope thermoelectric generators can no longer provide power.

Till then, should the discs be retrieved by beings from other planets, they will find photos of the earth and its life forms, greetings from the President of the United States as well as the Secretary-General of the UN, music by Mozart, Blind Willie Johnson, and Chuck Berry, and your name.

Let yours be the fifth face on Mount Rushmore, and below it, your name.

Let the four faces on Mount Rushmore be dynamited to pebbles and dust. Let yours alone appear there and the mountain be named for you.

Let your name be lisped by nuns saying their rosaries and priests telling their pater nosters.

Let it be on every prayer wheel, be it powered by wind, fire, water, or the hand of the devoted.

Let your name be such that when the sun streams through your window and you prepare to meet the day, flights of angels shall sing thee to thy single or double espresso, thy latte or cappuccino, thy tea of so many types that it would be impossible to enumerate them all, each more musical-sounding than the next, from chai and matcha to rosehip, spearmint, mulberry.

Let your name be such that each morning the devil says goddammit, she's up.

Foreign Movies

> Movies almost always had happy endings, unless they were foreign.
> —Andrew Grant Jackson, *1965: The Most Revolutionary Year in Music*

What's with you foreigners? We don't like that downer crap over here.
Oh, wait, we do: when the Shangri-Las recorded "The Leader of the Pack"
in 1964, it shot to the top of the *Billboard* Hot 100, and not because
Jimmy and his girl Betty rode off together on his motorcycle and lived
happily ever after, either, since her folks were always putting him down
(down, down) and saying he came from the wrong side of town,
so when she had to say goodbye, all she could do was cry, I'm sorry

I hurt you, the Leader of the Pack—easy words to sing, surely, though
getting all that pain across is another matter altogether, which is why,
before Jimmy rides off to get killed as lead singer Mary Weiss
sings "Look out! Look out! Look out!" producer Jeff Barry has to psych her up
until she bursts into tears at the story of the tough biker
who's really a softie at heart and the girl who somehow knows she'll never
see him again. Right now I'm the only customer in this restaurant,

meaning I have time to think that surely none of us is in favor of tragedy
as depicted in "The Leader of the Pack," the best-known example
of the teenage road death song (also called "death disc"
and "splatter platter"). But while on the surface it sounds like a song
for a girl audience, it's really a song for guys: masculine self-pity has
sold more records than any other emotion. Mainly, it's about
thwarted love, and every member of every audience has felt that.

I sip coffee and think, they like to cry, the people. To them, sorrow is a drug
or *pharmakon,* as the old Greeks had it, both remedy and poison, like
alcohol, which makes us happy but then stupid, or football, which builds
character—you get knocked down, you get back up—yet scrambles our brains.
My friend Erica Bernheim says,"I would like motorcycles so much better if they
didn't exist." You could say the same for thwarted love, yet who among us
has not had his or her heart broken, and who does not think that he or she

is a much better him or her as a result of that experience, even though
he or she didn't especially enjoy it at the time? According to Blake,
"If the doors of perception were cleansed every thing would appear to man
as it is, Infinite. For man has closed himself up, till he sees all things thro'
narrow chinks of his cavern." Maybe foreign movies are right to end unhappily.
Is Jimmy going to sweep Betty up and marry her and have a bunch
of greaser kids and start a successful chain of motorcycle sales

and repair shops, or is he going to run a stop sign and be turned into
hamburger by some sleep-deprived trucker in an 18-wheel rig?
You just don't know. I'm still the only customer in this restaurant,
but as I'm settling up, the door flies open, and eight sunburned golfers
fall through it, and it's obvious that they've already served themselves
liberally at the clubhouse's "nineteenth hole," so I ask the waitress if
she's ready for this, and she says, "I'm never ready. I just go with it."

My Girlfriend Killed James Brown

Guy walks up to me in the park and says, "My girlfriend killed
  James Brown," and I start to say, "Do I know you?" but
I don't want to miss out on the story, so I say, "No lie!" and he says,
  "Yeah, I got bumped up to first class, and when I saw who
my seatmate was, I went back to economy and told my girlfriend,
  and even though she had the flu, we switch places, and three

weeks later, James Brown is dead." How'd you like that on your résumé?
  Or anyone's death, though that didn't bother the local woman
who got life recently for murdering her husband because, according
  to the trial transcript, she didn't want to "suffer the shame of
a divorce." Nothing good comes from murder. Well, if you murder
  Hitler, yeah, but suppose you murder Hitler and somebody

worse takes his place? The girlfriend didn't mean to kill James Brown,
  though. Accidental death's a whole other kettle of fish. Imagine
the girlfriend sometime later on another flight, and she dozes off
  in the middle of a movie, and when she wakes, she notices
everyone else is sleeping, including the flight attendants, and she rings
  the call button, but nobody comes, and she shakes her seatmate's

arm, but he doesn't respond, either, and that's when she thinks,
  These people aren't sleeping, but the plane keeps flying, and
it lands somehow, and she finds herself at an arrival gate and then
  a cab stand, and she doesn't know where she wants to go, though
the cabbie seems to, and everyone is happy and friendly, if a little
  distant, she says to herself, *as though they're in this place but not*

really of it, and here she is finally in a room with white walls and statues
  in niches and portraits of people she doesn't recognize and a floor
that's lit from beneath, and people have cups of tea and finger sandwiches,
  and they're ordinary people, for the most part, but Otis is there,
and Sam Cooke, and Aretha, and someone taps her on the shoulder
  and says, "Try these," and she turns and puts her hand to her mouth

and begins to cry and says, "Oh, Mr. Brown, I'm so sorry I killed you,"
and he says, "That's okay, baby. I'm better now. I'm glad
I'm here. I feel good. Take a cookie. Take a macaroon," and she says,
"What about the jam thumbprints? Are they good, too?"
and he's saying "It's all good here, baby," and she says, "I'll just
have one—I don't want to spoil my appetite. What time's

dinner?" and he says, "Baby, we don't believe in that," and she says,
"You don't believe in dinner?" and he says, "No, time. We stopped
that long ago," and she says, "Who did? How?" and he says,
"Fats did when he sang 'Walking to New Orleans.' Tina stopped
time when she sang 'Fool in Love.' Buddy Holly did it with
'Not Fade Away,' same way Mozart did with that night music thing,"

and she says, "Mr. Brown, you know a lot more about classical music
than I would have thought" and then "You wouldn't happen to
be familiar with a 1956 French opera called *Dialogues of the Carmelites,*
would you?" and he says, "Know it? I wrote that shit," and she
says, "You did not—that was Francis Poulenc!" and he says, "Time don't
stop for one person. One person stops time. Somebody comes

in contact with what you've done, they catch some of that. That's the way
it works. One by one, them sixteen nuns stepped up to the guillotine,
and one by one them revolutionaries cut their heads off, so there were
fifteen singing, then fourteen, then none. Silence can be louder than
anything, you know. The sound of silence," says James Brown.
"And what is 'It's a Man's Man's Man's World' if not classical?

Full orchestra score, dark tones, nuanced lyrics: that fat Italian motherfucker
knocked it over the centerfield wall every time," and just then a voice
says, "Who you calling 'fat'?" and James Brown says, "Oh, sorry, Luciano.
Have a cookie. Okay, have all the cookies" as a man steps into the room
and says, "Brown, party of two," and James Brown gives her his arm,
and they go in, but the dining room is the kitchen she grew up in,

and her parents are sitting at the table, her father in a jacket and tie
and her mother in a pretty dress and that bright red lipstick she adored,

and they smile and wave, but they don't really seem to know her,
    either, and she says, "Holy cow! This looks like the house I grew up in!
Is this the house I grew up in?" as Janis Joplin scurries through
    with a tray on her shoulder and says, "Get up off of that thing, James"

and James Brown says, "Take another little piece of my heart, sis,"
    as Janis disappears into the kitchen, and her parents look up again,
and this time her mother says, "Darling, is that you?" and her dad says,
    "That's her, Miriam. Here, honey, have a seat," and she sits and says,
"Mom, Dad—how'd I get here?" and James Brown turns
    back to the woman who killed him and says, "You never left."

The 1909 Air Show at Brescia

Together, we imagined the future: D'Annunzio, Puccini,
Kafka, and all of us nobodies, you in your sack coat

and necktie and bowler, I in a skirt and shirtwaist and a hat
with a little brim that shaded my face. The pilots, too,

wore ordinary clothes. The planes were unloaded
and assembled where we could see them, and when they started,

they sounded like cars. When they went up, we saw them
the whole time as well, and when they came down,

they landed on bicycle wheels. But the planes knew more
than we did. We wanted the planes to be ideas

and they were, noisily considering the skies and then
remaking them according to their desires:

within a year, they flew above a thousand meters
at a speed of a hundred kilometers an hour.

We thought statesmen would fly to each other's countries
and explain themselves, but instead they built more planes,

added machine guns and bomb racks, turned the air
into battlefields. Still, we wanted to fly, not in some

rattletrap that spattered you with hot oil
but in a shiny tube that sped above the clouds

as attendants brought us cocktails, peanuts, dinner.
That night, we took the train back to Verona.

I heated a risotto, you grilled two beef cheeks and opened
a bottle of Amarone, and as I brought food to the table,

you took the cushions off the couch and piled them
on our chairs, joking that we were ahead

of the others, that we alone would know
what it's like to be above the world as we dined.

There'd been a strange innocence to the whole day, I said.
You said the things you love can kill you.

Then Elvis Drops to One Knee

I'm talking to Elvis's stepbrother, Rick Stanley,
and he's saying that when his daddy died, his mother put him
in foster care, but his foster parents were awful people
who held him down and poured Tabasco in his mouth
when he was bad or they thought he was, and then one day

his mother pulls up in a car with his new daddy,
and off they go to 3764 South Bellevue Road in Memphis,
to a place called Graceland, and everybody gets out
of the car, and Rick's walking around, and he ends up
in what's called the music room, and there's this guy

standing by the record player, and he's tall and slim
and has this slicked-back hair, and Rick has no idea
who he is. Help seems to arrive in the nick of time,
doesn't it? Churchy folk are taught to pray for it,
to teach others to pray: a bird that had learned

to speak was being chased by a hawk, and when it cried,
"Saint Thomas, help me!" the hawk fell dead, and the bird
flew on. If you don't love the Catholic Church,
there's something wrong with you. Still, what about the hawk?
What if the bird were a bad bird and the hawk a good one?

What if the bird were so bad that no other bird would
have him, were covetous, adulterous, gluttonous,
and so on, whereas the hawk was hardworking
and had a family to take care of and tithed 10 percent
of the birds he caught to the poor and indigent hawks,

the disabled, the ones who couldn't hunt for themselves?
How kind it is to help others. Yesterday my boy Darrell

Bourque read poems by Donne, Shakespeare, Countee Cullen,
and Yusef Komunyakaa to a community of retired Jesuits
in Grand Coteau, LA, and today he sent me this note:

"There were about fifteen residents of the retirement facility
that came to the reading yesterday, ages sixty-five to one hundred.
Some of them drift off as I read, some never make eye contact,
some smile from beginning to end. But they love poetry,
just as I love these lovely human beings who have led

directed, purposeful lives and are now in these latter stages
of unfolding. The one-hundred-year-old wanted to know if I could
recommend some really good atheist poets."
What if we prayed for the wrong things? And got them.
You don't have to be a priest to be a good person.

Just be kind. That way, you'll answer someone else's prayers,
and the other person doesn't even have to pray to have
their prayers answered. In the music room, Rick Stanley
is just standing there, and Elvis looks at him and walks over
and drops to one knee and says, "Ah always wanted a little brother."

Racing through Pittsburgh with Annie Dillard

The Catholic Church *hated* perspective, I mean *hated* it
because it distorted the distances between objects,
as the Catholic Church saw it, not that the Church itself
didn't make a change or two to the normal view of how
things work. Let's start with virgin birth—let's end there
as well, because this poem is not a polemic against
the Catholic Church but an attempt to discover a rule

or rules for establishing the best distance between one's
self and the thing that one wishes to master, appreciate,
avoid, and so on, depending on whether or not that thing
is your enemy, your baby doll, your lunch, the guy who
bullied you in high school, a mime who is mocking someone else
(which is funny) or you (which is not), a fire on a cold night.
Author Annie Dillard could certainly tell you that there's

a right distance for everything, recalling in her memoir
her tomboy days in Pittsburgh when she played tackle
football with boys and, one day during a blizzard,
pelted a passing car with snowballs and was chased
ten blocks by the driver through alleys and backyards
while feeling no fear, even when she was caught along
with a kid named Mikey. It was as though she'd won

an Olympic medal, she remembers. What could the guy
do? Nothing that mattered. "If he had cut off our heads,"
Dillard remembers, "I would have died happy,"
but the man just said, "You stupid kids," and went back
to his car. The chase was a challenge, an honor, something
that should happen to every kid and that every kid wants,
whether he or she knows it or not, which is why I always

shout at kids when I see them fooling around outside
my window. "You stupid kids get out of my yard!"

I shout. "Get out of my yard or I'll grab a stick
and knock your brains out!" They're poking at something,
a dead animal or an anthill, and they look up when
I yell and then at each other and they haul ass down
the street to their own houses, to the next year of school

and an uncertain future. Sometimes the best distance
is no distance, and here I am thinking of the hiker
who has been told, when a bear approaches, to drop
into a fetal position so that the bear can sniff him or her,
affirm his or her harmlessness, and shuffle off toward
its berry bush or honey hive or whatever it is that
the bear prefers to the human flesh in which it is no longer

interested. I don't care what the Catholic Church says,
its magnificent cathedrals and often overlooked
compassion for the poor and the sick notwithstanding:
in art, perspective is crucial. People say the proportions
of Michelangelo's *David* are all wrong because the statue
was originally intended to be placed on top of the Duomo,
meaning that certain parts of the sculpture would have

to be accentuated in order to be visible below, though
one wonders if this asymmetry may simply be due
to the demands of the stone. When the Temptations sing
"I Can't Get Next to You," what they're really saying
is that the "you" in the song doesn't really want
the "I" to get any closer than he is already,
which rejection the "I" should take in stride, since,

as my nephew said to his father when that father
was complaining that he'd been turned down by yet
another woman in a long line of women who had
turned him down and for good reason, though we needn't
go into that here, "Dad, if they don't like you, what's
the point?" Okay, but try telling that to the Temptations.
Take it from me, Temptations: it's only going

to work if she wants you as much as you want her.
The dog can't catch the car—what would the dog do
if it caught the car? The *David* has to step down from
its pedestal and show you how to find the right stone,
how to put it in the sling and whirl that sling over
your head without braining yourself and release one end
at just the right moment, Goliath looking on like the big

dumb oaf he is as the stone gets closer and closer, then
pow, right in the kisser. People, get ready, in the words
of the late Curtis Mayfield, another Motown genius, because
the world is coming at us a mile a minute, though it doesn't
know what it's doing any more than we do. Over here,
world! It's me, squatting down in my catcher's stance,
no chest protector, mask, shin guards, just this glove.

Europeans Wrapping Knickknacks

They're so meticulous, aren't they? They take such care
that I am ashamed for my country, that impatient farm boy,
that factory hand with the sausage fingers. First there's
the fragile object itself—vase, jewel, ornament—then tissue,
stiff paper, bubble wrap, tissue again, tape, a beautiful bag
made from something more like gift wrap than the stern brown
stuff we use here in the States, then the actual carry bag

that has a little string handle but which is, in many ways,
the loveliest part of the package except for the object
you can barely remember, it's been so long since
you've seen it. In America, we just drop your trinket
in a sack and hand it to you. Oh, that's right. We have cars
in this country: whereas Stefano or Nathalie has to elbow his
or her way down a crowded street and take the bus or subway,

you get in the car, put the bag on the seat next to you,
and off you go, back to your bungalow in Centralia or Eau Claire.
Of course, this doesn't mean you're culturally inferior
to Jacques or Magdalena just because, as Henry James
said in his book-length essay on Hawthorne, we have no sovereign
in our country, no court, no aristocracy, no high church,
no palaces or castles or manors, no thatched cottages,

no ivied ruins. No, we just do things differently here:
whereas Pedro and Ilsa take the tram or trolley,
you have your car, and now you're on your way home
to Sheboygan or Dearborn, probably daydreaming
as you turn the wheel, no more aware of your surroundings
than 53-year-old Michael Stepien was in 2006 when
he was walking home after work in Pittsburgh, which

is when a teenager robbed him and shot him in the head,
and as Mr. Stepien lay dying, his family decided
"to accept the inevitable," said his daughter Jeni,
and donate his heart to one Arthur Thomas
of Lawrenceville, NJ, who was within days of dying.
That's one thing you can say about life in the US:
we have great medicine. Mr. Thomas recovered nicely

after the transplant, and he and the Stepiens
kept in touch, swapping holiday cards and flowers
on birthdays. And then Jeni Stepien gets engaged to be
married and thinks, Who will walk me down the aisle?
No cathedrals in America, says Henry James,
no abbeys, no little Norman churches, no Oxford or Eton
or Harrow, no sporting class, no Epsom nor Ascot.

"Some such list as that might be drawn up of the absent
things in American life," says James, "the effect of which,
upon an English or a French imagination, would probably
as a general thing be appalling." It gets worse: James then
says, "The natural remark, in the almost lurid light of such
an indictment, would be that if these things are left out,
everything is left out," but then "the American knows that

a good deal remains; what it is that remains—that is
his secret." As the wedding approaches, Jeni Stepien
thinks, book the venue? Check. Order the cake? Got it.
And then she thinks that it would be incredible to have
her father there one way or another, so she writes Mr. Thomas,
who says yes, of course, he'll be happy to walk her down
the aisle, though when he says he's afraid his emotions

might get the better of him, Jeni tells him hers might, too,
but not to worry, because "I'll be right there with you."
When they finally meet, Arthur Thomas suggests

that Jeni grip his wrist, where the pulse is strongest:
"I thought that would be the best way for her to feel close
to her dad," he says. "That's her father's heart beating."
At the wedding, Jeni is photographed with her hand

on Arthur's chest. They dance together, the guests mingle,
the two families vow to meet up somewhere down the road,
Jeni and her husband start their new life together,
and Arthur Thomas returns to his home in Lawrenceville.
"I felt wonderful about bringing her dad's heart to Pittsburgh
that day," he says. "If I'd had to, I would've walked."
Talk about a knickknack. What must it be like

to have someone else's heart in your chest,
taken from his body years earlier and placed in yours,
beating there now as it beat for its owner. You were days
from death, and now you can do anything you want.
In your new life, you are a citizen of no country
but of the world. It's your heart. Your secret.
Most days you don't even know it's there.

Ode to My Skinny Legs

When you look up "man of parts," you get the eighteenth-century definition
of that term, meaning someone who is capable in multiple endeavors,
though if you look up "woman of parts," you get a lot of websites
dealing with anatomy. Very unfair! as the president of the United States
would say. And not just the president: anyone can see that it never was,

is not, and never will be right to define men by their big brains
and women by their bodies, not that brains aren't body parts.
"Everybody loves their own body," I heard a woman say recently,
and the man who was with her said, "It's a love-hate relationship,
isn't it?" Well, yes and no. I mean, you can give your body the finger,

but you'd be using at least one part of your body to tell the rest of it
to get lost. Also, don't we feel differently about our bodies during
different times of our life? A fifteen-year-old who sees a single hair
on her leg will want to shave that leg immediately so that no one
will know she's an animal, that is, a human like the rest of us,

whereas ten years later the same person will go for days or even
a lifetime without shaving, figuring eh, big deal, who cares,
we're all gonna die anyway. You can't tickle yourself, but you can
give yourself a high five. And you should! You and your body
have got this far, and you did it together. Take me, for example.

Nobody has skinnier legs than I do. They resemble nothing more
than "two rat tails hanging out of a cracker box," to use my high
school football coach's accurate if less than totally complimentary
description of my nether appendages. They're not my legs
anyway, since I got them from my dad—if you think my legs

are skinny, Coach Wilson, you should have seen T. A. Kirby's!
Yet just as his took him all over the US for eighty-eight years, not to mention

Germany, France, England, Italy, and Portugal, so mine have taken
    me to those same countries and to Russia, India, and Japan as well,
and not just across the flat surfaces, either, but up and over assorted peaks,

pinnacles, promontories, parapets, and campaniles, which actions
    have not only given me a great deal of satisfaction in the moment
but also made it possible for me to eat whatever I wanted on
    the evenings of the days on which those actions took place, since
the exertion undertaken in each instance more than compensated

for the subsequent caloric intake. Why, just this morning they took
    me all the way to the top of the Duomo, which is 463 steps, not
counting all the steps it took to get me to the church in the first place
    as well as those I took afterward as I staggered around Florence
in agony. Still, I was with a dozen students who were breathing

as hard as I was, though I have no idea if their quads, hamstrings,
    and calf muscles are as sore as mine are right now. Probably not.
And these same legs have also taken me over the little bridges
    of Venice, any number of which are not so little and rather steep,
in point of fact, as well as in and out of the many beautiful churches

of that city as well, including the church of the Frari where Titian
    is buried and where I hear a guide tell a group of tourists that
the great artist was said to be ninety when he died, although,
    since no one knows when he was born, we should say he was "more
or less ninety." Aren't we all more or less ninety? Enrico Dandolo

was ninety and blind when he was the doge of Venice in the twelfth
    and thirteenth centuries, yet he kicked ass, including but not limited
to Venetian ass as well as the asses, butts, bondoons, tuchuses,
    rumps, sterns, fannies, posteriors, backsides, and whoopee cakes
of assorted Greeks, Croats, Byzantines, Bulgarians, Slavs, Istrians,

and Dalmatians, by which latter term I mean not the endearing
    pooches associated with firetrucks and some of your more cloying

Walt Disney productions but the citizens of Dalmatia, a narrow belt
of land on the east shore of the Adriatic Sea stretching from the island
of Rab in the north to the Bay of Kotor in the south, and the sworn

enemies of Venice, at least until such time as they were not.
And therefore I declare that I am completely satisfied with my entire
body in its every aspect, including my skinny legs, although,
as I've said, they're not really mine, since I got them from my dad—
he was just taking care of them for me till I came along.

High School

It would have been a joke if prisons were jokes.
We read the usual in English class—Steinbeck,
Hemingway—and our science teachers meant well,
but for all they taught us, we might have lived
in the eighteenth century, when universities focused
mainly on theology, and science was conducted

on weekends by gentlemen with hand-cranked
electrostatic generators and butterfly nets. As far as
social studies, forget it: the teacher scolded me
when he didn't know who the Chief Justice was and I did,
and when he tried to say *quiet,*
it came out *quite. Be quite, Kirby! Bertrand and Kirby,*

be quite now! The girls were beautiful.
I was sixteen. Even the plain girls were beautiful.
But they didn't know how to kiss, and I didn't know
how to teach them. About that time, the folk music
craze hit, and when the Kingston Trio's *Close Up*
dropped in October of that year, Al Edwards

and Bob Spain and I figured the road to glory
was paved with sheet music, and since Al already
owned a guitar and Bob a banjo, that left the bongos
to me, it remaining only for our mothers to starch
and iron our look-alike shirts, white half-sleeved
affairs with blue stripes that appeared to be made out

of the cloth usually reserved for window awnings,
the kind of shirts worn only by hot dog
vendors and folk singers, meaning they were the kind
the Kingston Trio would have worn had they been us.
After we played our first show in the cafeteria,
four of the bustiest girls in our school ran up

and squealed, "You sound exactly like the Trio!"
What were they talking about? None of us could
sing at all. We should have practiced more
and squabbled less. The best thing you could say
about us is that we didn't forget any of the words
and that we more or less began and ended together.

Other than that, we were terrible. I'd never been
happier in my life. We played another dozen dates
or so, and then Al's uncle proposed he take us
on the road for the summer to play in the school gyms
of towns so isolated that people who couldn't make it
to Vicksburg or Montgomery to hear real musicians

might actually pay to hear us. But our mothers said no;
they gave no reasons, but I'm guessing
they saw us falling into the clutches of hard women, desperate
small-town divorcées who'd introduce us to cigarettes,
underage drinking, and worse.
I wanted worse. I wanted to kiss an older woman, somebody

who was twenty-eight, say, even thirty, a blonde
in capri pants and heels, her top sliding off
one shoulder, her smoky breath in my face
and then her lips on mine like a hot wind, the one desert dwellers
call *samoon,* which means *poison*
because others drop dead at its approach, but not me,

who is wrapped by it, lifted, my mouth sprung
by a kiss like lightning, a flash that spreads and spreads
and stays as I feel each thing that will
happen in my life from this moment on, the way those wrecked
and under water follow a train of images
until they sink, and the darkness returns, and they're free.

Sally Go 'Round the Roses

In junior high, we all listened and danced to
and sang along with "Sally Go 'Round the Roses"
by the Jaynetts, but nobody knew what it meant.
The song told Sally not to go downtown, to stay
in the garden, that the roses won't tell her secret.
We didn't know anything about Sally or her secret,
though that didn't stop us from guessing. All we did
in those days was guess. At everything. Lisa Stuart
said when she looked at pictures of Keith Richards
of the Rolling Stones, she got "funny feelings,"
but when we asked her what they were, she couldn't say.
And didn't want to say, probably, any more than
we wanted to know what we desired and feared most.
We were like the last cave people to accept fire:
the other tribes had hot meals and light at night,
and we wanted that as well, but we were unsure.
We'd heard the Hill People wailing as their forest burned,
and someone said that Atouk had lost his hand.
But when the earth cooled, Myla used a charred stick
to tell the story of the blaze and the ones who survived it.
She brushed dirt off limestone and drew trees flowering
into fire, animals fleeing, hunters pursuing them
with club and spear. Then she turned to us
and smiled as if to say, see? From flames, art.

The Locomotion

Student's so tired she's weepy. *I just got off a double shift,*
she says, and I tell her not to worry, that we've all had
terrible jobs but things turn out okay, and then I tell her

about my worst job ever, which was building roads
in Claiborne Parish that summer, the sun itself hot enough,
the tar puddling around our boots like lava leaked

from Dante's hell. Jules LeBlanc and I bunked together
and drove back to Baton Rouge on the weekends
to do laundry and eat our mothers' cooking,

but on our last day before we went off to college,
we stopped at a roadhouse and emptied can after can
of Busch beer, the white mountains of the logo

holding out their snowy promise. Somehow
we made our way down Essen Lane, and when we stopped
at the first light and Little Eva's "Loco-Motion" came on,

Jules cranked the volume knob, whipped his hard hat
into the woods, stepped to the car behind us, dragged out
the driver and his wife, and said, *Okay, dance.*

Pope Leo X said, "Since God has given us the papacy,
let us enjoy it." I felt the same way about rock 'n' roll.
It gave me *somebodiness,* to use Dr. King's word.

As the song spooled out into the night, we shook
and shimmied, the old-timers and the two young idiots,
and then I looked over my shoulder and said,

Jules, your truck's rolling, and we took off down Essen,
    but just before Jules jumped through his door
and I through mine, I turned to check on the old folks.

Were they okay? asks my student. The light
    hadn't changed, I say. His arm was around her waist,
his other hand was in hers. They were still dancing.

Chasing Jim Taylor

When I ask the man with the streetside cooker for the secret
of his fried fish, he says *I use the same flour and oil*

and salt as everyone else, but they can't do with it
what I do, and as I drive past a group of kids playing ball

in a dusty lot, I ease the box open and nibble a fillet
and remember how my friends and I played football

in a neighbor's yard in junior high, and sometimes
this man came out of the house next door to scrimmage

with us, a big man who moved well, though he handed off
every play to one of us, and if he passed on a tip

from time to time, it was always in a *let's-try-this* way.
Even when he had the ball, somehow we always caught him.

Every half hour or so, a mother would step onto her porch,
arms folded across her chest, watch us for a while,

go back inside. Our moms kept other men away:
the youth minister who invited boys to his apartment

but never girls, the lifeguard instructor who made me
rescue him again and again as he laughed and flailed.

Napoleon said *An army without a general is just a group*
of frightened men. We weren't frightened, just clueless.

We wanted to run. We wanted to win. We didn't know
what we wanted. Once a journeyman guitar player said

There's a lot of people who can play better than me,
but they can't play with the Stones better than me.

Later I found out the big man was future Hall of Famer
Jim Taylor, who played fullback for the Green Bay Packers

and whose parents lived in the neighborhood.
Jim Taylor was getting us ready for a world that didn't

care about us. He wanted us to learn, not football,
but who we were. *Your tailbone should be lower than*

your shoulders, he said. *Don't watch the other guy's head.*
Watch his feet. This fish is delicious. The hushpuppies, too.

Jim Taylor taught us everything we needed to know.
Get the ball, he said. *Give it to someone else.*

A Momentary Lapse in Judgment

Ever have one? Me, neither. Well, yeah, my first marriage,
which didn't seem like a bad call at the time, but then
these things never do, do they? Sure, smoking while refueling
your car is stupid, as is getting out of that same car to embrace
a park bear on the assumption that all those Disney movies
you saw as a kid were documentaries and that park bears
will giggle if you tickle them and burst into song the second
an invisible orchestra begins to play. Then again, at times
every life unfolds like the so-called chain race you see
at small-town dirt tracks in which three cars are chained together,
and the front car, typically a Chevy that's seen better days,
has an engine and a driver but no brakes, and it's chained
to a driverless Yugo, and the Yugo is chained to a Ford Pinto
that has brakes and a driver but no engine, and around the cars
go on a figure-eight track as the drivers try to get to the finish line
ahead of the other drivers of one or more other sets of cars,
and the cars bang together and break down and catch fire
while the audience laughs and eats their wings and nachos
and wipes their greasy fingers on their t-shirts, and that's you
out there, you think, driving and braking at the same time,
because if life is complicated, humans are even more so.
But when you look back, doesn't your life look a lot less
like a wreckage-strewn infield and more like a finely crafted
novel? First you have to make your mistakes, though.
You know what they say: good judgment comes from
experience, and experience comes from bad judgment.
A young friend of mine says she has a crush on a guy
but is nervous about telling him because she doesn't want
to embarrass herself, but I tell her to just start writing him
without thinking about what she'll say, that she's smart,
she'll figure it out, or the words will figure it out for her.
Actually, my first wife and I had good times—a lot
of good times, come to think of it. Plus we've both been

remarried for decades, so maybe we had to go through
each other to get to the ones who were right for us.
Start overthinking everything and you may as well
go into the forest and ask the trees if they think they're
in the right place. Ask the warbler if he wouldn't rather
sing some Brahms, say, or Schubert. And that squirrel,
the one with the nut in her paws? Ask her if that's
the right nut. Tell her she'd be happier if she had another
nut instead. She'd look at you as though you're crazy.
She'd look at you, like, what kind of squirrel are you, man?

Hitchhike

Hell isn't endless suffering, says French philosopher
and political activist Simone Weil, it's endless monotony,
the same thing over and over again. Think Liverpool, think 1963,
and there you are: you married too young and you have too many
kids and either a dead-end job or no job and an ocean of beer
to drown it all in, and suddenly four guys from your neighborhood—

your neighborhood!—shout "Please Please Me" and "Love
Me Do" and "I Want to Hold Your Hand," and like that,
you're free: sure, the bills and backaches will still be there
in the morning, but you're free for two minutes and change,
and if you can be not simply your own person but something
like a god on this earth for these two minutes now, then why not

more tomorrow, the next day, the day after that? Just because
a song is fun doesn't mean that it can't be serious:
the Beatles are still in short pants when Little Richard
records "Tutti Frutti" in New Orleans. It's 1955 now,
and a year later, Allen Ginsberg writes "America" in Berkeley,
and if that "queer Jewish commie anarchist dope fiend can refuse

the internal exile his country has offered him," as cultural critic
Greil Marcus says of Ginsberg in his book *Mystery Train,*
then the gay black crippled anarchist dope fiend can do the same,
only with a drum kit and saxophones. Imagine a portrait
of the Founding Fathers, including the John Hancock whose
name is evoked daily as millions of patriotic Americans jack up

the gross national product by signing contracts, loan agreements,
and credit card slips for everything from a pack of cigarettes
to a new automobile, only this time Little Richard and Allen
Ginsberg are in the picture with their crazy hair and loopy
facial expressions, Richard with his arm around the shoulders
of a startled Button Gwinnett and Allen about to pinch

the bottom of Francis Lightfoot Lee, whose name, like
Gwinnett's, is itself the essence of both poetry and rock 'n' roll
and who has no idea what's about to happen. Ah, uncertainty!
How we fear and need you. Now picture these same men
nervously fingering their quill pens as they wonder whether
or not to sign the Declaration of Independence which will certainly

change their world and might even change the world as a whole
and is also a document that bolstered the citizens and soldiers
to whom it was read aloud, just as "Tutti Frutti" bolstered us
teenagers as we tried to figure out what we were doing, where
we were going, who we loved, who loved us. Younger reader,
that is, any reader of this poem who is younger than me, which,

come to think of it, is likely to be almost every reader, have I lost you
already? Your music and my music are not the same music.
My music is the artists and groups I have already named as well as
a thousand others—Jackie Wilson, the Clash, Otis, Etta,
Aretha, all doowop, most early rap/grunge/punk/psychobilly,
and, hovering over them all, beautiful doomed Marvin Gaye—

whereas yours consists of musicians I won't even try to name
because (a) I'll pick the wrong ones and (b) I'm certain that,
if what I've written here is read a month or a year or ten years from now,
the wheel will have turned by then, the seasons changed,
the sun risen and sunk and been unhorsed by the moon
and risen again, and musical tastes, too, will have evolved

so radically that what your children listen to will be as different from
your music as yours is from mine. Whoever your favorites are,
swear on a stack of 45s that you listen to them in your car. Young people's
music was meant to be listened to on Sunset Strip, Route 66,
the New Jersey turnpike, A1A all the way from Jacksonville
to the Keys, and the best songs all have cars in them,

from Robert Johnson's "Terraplane Blues" to Chuck Berry's
"Maybellene" to Janis Joplin's "Mercedes Benz" and Tracy

Chapman and pretty much everything by Springsteen and the Beach Boys.
        But say you don't have a car or don't have a car that works
                or do have a car but someone else has borrowed/stolen/wrecked it:
you can still stick out your thumb and get picked up by some stranger

who will take you where you want to go or, if you're really lucky,
                to someplace you've never heard of but that's better than where
you were going in the first place. Of course, that same person
        may saw your head off and leave it by the side of the road
                and the rest of you in a dumpster behind the Waffle House in
the next town, because that kind of thing does happen from time to time,

but it happens a lot less often than the other thing, and besides,
                you're not looking for something anymore but someone and not just
anyone, either, you're looking for the one who will do for you
        what a great song or a great poem does and free you, turn you
                into a god, take you off your feet and away from home, then lead you
back, and not just for the time it takes you to listen or read but forever,

and besides, a car has just pulled over, and the engine's idling,
                and you look through the window, and the driver has a half smile
and is chewing on a toothpick or a stick of gum or maybe
        a sliver of his last passenger's soul, and you think *I'm going*
                to do this and then *I'd have to be crazy to do this* and then *I've got*
to find that girl if I have to hitchhike around the world.

This Magic Moment

Poetry does make things happen. A friend says, "I wanted
to let you know that my stepfather is chattering like
a schoolboy about a poem of yours on my Facebook page.
This may not seem like much to you, but this guy has been
giving me a hard time since I was two. You built a bridge
between people who never understood each other before."
How'd that happen? Magic, that's how. I know the poem

she means; it took me years to write it. Songwriter
Doc Pomus was crippled by polio, and he wrote once
about this dream he had again and again: "I used to believe
in magic and flying and that one morning I would wake up
and all the bad things were bad dreams. . . . And I would
get out of the wheelchair and walk and not with braces
and not with crutches," though when the light came through

the window in the morning, there he was, encased
in steel and leather from hip to ankle, unable to move.
Again and again he has the dream, and then one day
he writes "This Magic Moment," where the guy meets
the girl, and suddenly he has everything he wants. How?
Magic! Wouldn't you love to have saved pale Keats
with his blood-speck'd lips? And Fanny, her skin like cream,

listening through the wall. He dies with his lungs on fire,
she mourns, marries, gives birth, and, after her husband dies,
gives Keats's letters to her children—she had kept them all
that time. We have them, and we have his poems. And his
tool kit, too: look what he does in the "Ode to a Nightingale."
Nobody bolts music and lyrics together the way Keats does,
no one pays more attention to detail. There's a Jack Gilbert

poem that begins with a real incident from World War II,
when the Polish cavalry rode out against the Germans
with their swords glittering, only the Germans had tanks.
But that's not bravery, says Gilbert. Bravery is doing
the same thing every day when you don't want to.
Not the marvelous but the familiar, over and over again.
Do that, and the magic will come. My dad was frail

and distracted in his last hours. My mother said he asked,
Do we have enough money? and when she said yes, he said,
Then let's just get in the Buick and go. He was looking
at car trips, thirty-cent gas, roadside picnics, these new things
they called motels. My brother, me, the little house
we lived in, fifty years of marriage, a long and happy life as
a Chaucer scholar: all that was in the sunny days to come.

To My Body

I'm listening to a lecture on W. E. Henley, author of "Invictus," the poem that ends "I am the master of my fate, / I am the captain of my soul,"
when the lecturer notes that Henley underwent the amputation of his left leg when he was barely out of his teens and, after his recovery,
worked as a journalist, writing on society and current events and trying to be
a bohemian or, as the lecturer says, "as much as you can be a bohemian on one leg,"
and I think, can't you be a bohemian on one leg as well as two? After all, a bohemian is little more than someone who lives an unconventional
and more or less artistic lifestyle. As far as I can tell, there's no requirement regarding a certain number of legs.

Henley's great friend was Robert Louis Stevenson, who wore his hair long and favored velveteen jackets and thus was something
of a bohemian himself, though he wrote the most unbohemian novel ever, namely,
Treasure Island, a tale of manly men if ever there was one, including the pirate Long John Silver, whose physical description is based on the person of, that's right, W. E. Henley.
Stevenson's stepson said Henley was "a great, glowing, massive-shouldered fellow with a big red beard and a crutch; jovial, astoundingly clever,
and with a laugh that rolled like music; he had an unimaginable fire and vitality; he swept one off one's feet,"
and after *Treasure Island* was published, Stevenson himself wrote Henley and said, "I will now make a confession: It was the sight of your maimed strength
and masterfulness that begot Long John Silver . . . the idea of the maimed man, ruling and dreaded by the sound, was entirely taken from you."
That settles that, then. You can be a bohemian with one leg and probably no legs at all, should it come to that.

Here's another puzzler for you: when you hear someone say, "My fiancé is in New York" or "I just was talking to my fiancée, and she said such and so," why is it that you always look at him or her and say to yourself, "Wow, lucky fellow" or "Wait, *you* have a fiancée?"

If you paid attention to everything everybody said, you'd go crazy, but whenever you hear somebody use the word "fiancé" or "fiancée," you can't help looking at them.

Already I'm tired of the extra "e." Why can't other languages be as dumb as ours.

Also, what's the point of getting engaged? When I asked Barbara to marry me,

I said, "Would you rather have a big ring or go to Paris?" and she said, "Où est mon valise!"

Next thing you know, we are tramping down the Boulevard Saint-Germain and up the Boulevard Saint-Michel and sampling oysters, mussels, prawns, lobsters, and squid, gazing deeply into each other's eyes as we do so.

"To turn from everything to one face is to find oneself face to face with everything," said Elizabeth Bowen.

Boy, were you ever right about that, Elizabeth. Unless, of course, it's Jean-Paul Sartre's face.

Camus saw Sartre over-wooing a pretty girl and wondered why he didn't play it cool, as Camus himself would have.

"You've seen my face?" Sartre answered. And he's not the only one: James Baldwin is famous for saying, "I could talk away my looks in ten minutes,"

and Prufrock thinks, "There will be time, there will be time / To prepare a face to meet the faces that you meet"

or to don the invisible mask, as David Bowie called it: the story goes that the pop star was meeting a group of schoolchildren,

and one especially is shy and withdrawn, so Bowie says he'll meet with him separately, and he tells the boy he's wearing an invisible mask

and says, "I always feel afraid, just the same as you, but I wear this mask every day," and he takes his invisible mask off

and gives it to the boy and spins another mask out of nothing and says, "Now we've both got invisible masks,

and no one knows we're wearing them." And the boy, who is now the man telling the story,

says, "It was the first time I felt safe in my whole life." Feeling safe: that's the thing, isn't it?

Another person, whether he or she be a fiancé or fiancée or something else entirely, makes us feel as though we'll never be lonely and afraid again,
that we are indeed the captains of our souls.

W. E. Henley had a daughter, Margaret, who was beloved by all and sundry, including another writer who was at least as famous
as Robert Louis Stevenson, and Margaret called this other writer her "friendy," but she couldn't pronounce her Rs,
so the word came out as "fwendy" and often "fwendy-wendy," whence the name "Wendy Darling," protagonist of,
that's right, *Peter Pan,* J. M. Barrie's classic adventure tale for kids of all ages—immortal adventure tale, I should say,
since *Peter Pan* will always be loved by its readers as well as fans of its myriad stage and film versions.

Art is long, life is short, say the old Romans. Margaret Henley's life was certainly short; she was sickly at birth and died at the age of five.
Our bodies have a lot to answer for, don't they? They're so careless! They lose their parts or they expire abruptly or they're simply displeasing to the eyes, our own as well as the eyes of others.
Though when our bodies work right, they give us so much pleasure.
Amy Schumer calls an orgasm "the one good thing we're allowed as humans." Ha, ha!
Truer words, Amy, truer words! Though pecan pie is a close second.

O body, when you were five, you were hospitalized with polio.
O body, you wore braces and then you took them off, but look how skinny your legs are to this day.
O body, your owner played sports in high school, none well.
O body, how you love to eat! O body, you love soul food best because that is what you grew up on,
but you also love food of every kind, from chili dogs to foie gras and warm goat cheese salad.
O body, they say we should dance as though no one is looking, and you do, even though everyone is looking.
O body, you remind me every day to apply sunblock with an SPF of 50 or higher

and to reapply it after I shout, "Can opener!" and jump in the pool in my baggy board shorts,
frightening the children whose bodies their mommies clasp to their own so the little tykes won't be afraid of the loud man in the baggy board shorts.

O body, you love to watch every kind of movie, from popcorn movies to gloomy indie flicks set in locales visited only by filmmakers, like Anatolia.
O body, you love to listen to every kind of music in the record store, from early baroque to psychobilly and crust punk,
though you are happiest in the aisle marked "Early Rhythm 'n' Blues," bluegrass not so much.

O body, you make jokes, even if they don't always work, and in this you show humility, because the joke is always on you.
O body, you love alcohol—you loved it in great quantities once, but now you love it even more in small ones.
O body, you love LSD and mescaline, coke and weed not so much.
O body, the body of your father lived to be eighty-eight and that of your mother to ninety-nine, meaning you are likely to live a good long time yourself.
O body, what will you do if you live that long?
O body, let's hope it's possible for old people to use heroin then.

O body, I don't sleep as well as I'd like to, but when I wake up in the middle of the night,
I always say a little prayer of thanks to you, my body, for being there to keep me company until I doze off again.
And when I wake, the first thing I do is touch you to make sure you're still there, and you always are.

O body, you gaze upon the major as well as the minor artworks, from the refrigerator scrawls of nieces and nephews
to the masterpieces of the Uffizi and the Louvre, and once you took the train to Orvieto
to look at Luca Signorelli's frescoes that show the body doing everything a body can do:
rise to heaven with the angels, descend to hell with the demons, sell itself in the marketplace to lewd old men

yet mainly be born again, emerging from the earth as a bony skeleton that puts
on its body as though it were a costume.
O body, you are my fiancé, for we are two or I wouldn't be addressing you this
way, yet we are one.
O body, we will go to the grave together.
O body, you are an atheist, yet you thank God every day.

A Baby in the Piazza

What's the difference between Eisenhower-era horror movies
and the Italian Renaissance? Not a whole lot, I think to myself
as I cross the piazza after a night of drinking with friends,
and suddenly a wolf tears past, the moon rises and sets
and rises again, clouds race across the sky, vines snake up trees,

temple columns, the legs of passersby as the fog rolls over
the low wall that separates the river from the city, down
the galleries and alleyways until it covers the cars, the buildings,
the people who feel as though they've been blindfolded
and spun about in a children's game, and there's a long silence,

the tolling of a bell—one, two, three—then more silence still,
and, from somewhere in the mist, the cry of a baby.
Even the statues seem to hear it: Judith pauses as she cuts off
the head of Holofernes, David turns away from Goliath,
and Perseus looks in bewilderment at the head of Medusa

as it, too, turns left and right, mouth opening and closing
silently, like a monster in one of those horror movies I loved
as a kid: *Cannibal Holocaust, Bloodsucking Freaks, City
of the Living Dead.* Perseus is the mightiest work of the most
mighty of sculptors, the Benvenuto Cellini who, when

his own powers wane, summons those of the underworld:
in Rome he falls hard for a Sicilian girl named Angelica,
but when her mother gets wind of his plans, she spirits
the girl back to Sicily. Beside himself, Cellini hires a priest
who has a reputation as a conjurer of demons, and off they go

to the Colosseum along with several other sketchy
characters as well as the one figure the priest insists

is necessary to the rite, "a little boy of pure virginity,"
which is how I might have described myself as a young
moviegoer had I been familiar with the word "virginity."

Not all the films I saw as a kid were of the-gore-the-merrier
type. Some were downright silly, like *Thankskilling,* in which
the killer is a talking turkey who wears the teen protagonists'
dead dad's face, though no one seems to notice. And then
there was *The Tingler,* which was about a parasite in the human

body that fed on fear, the idea being that you should see
a scary movie and try not to get scared. The theater seats were
wired to vibrate, and ads promised that nurses would be on duty
in the aisles, and there they were, five women with upswept hair
and starched uniforms. It would be years before I looked back

and thought how hard-faced those nurses were, how they
smoked cigarettes and chewed gum, how little they were
like the nurses at the doctor's office, and I began to wonder
if they didn't make their living some other way, but then
sex was not on the menu yet for me, though it would be.

In the Colosseum, Cellini holds a pentagram over
the little boy's head while the others throw perfume
on the fire and chant in Greek, Latin, and Hebrew.
If Cellini had seen as many horror movies as I have,
he might have guessed that the ceremony would work

too well: thousands of demons appear and tell Cellini
that "in a month, you will be where Angelica is,"
only now what is he going to do about all those demons?
The little boy is shrieking in terror, saying, "This is
how I will meet death, for we are certainly dead men,"

which is a funny way for a kid to describe himself,
since he was no more a man than I was when I was his age,

though I was beginning to get interested in the things
men liked, such as women, and my taste in films changed
accordingly, leading me to *Piranha 3-D,* for example,

which probably contains the only 3-D boobs-bouncing-
underwater scene ever filmed, and *Ilsa, She-Wolf of the SS,*
the protagonist of which is a camp commandant
who rapes a male prisoner every night and punishes him
with castration and death when he ejaculates.

A single prisoner, an American, can avoid ejaculating,
and it is he who leads the successful revolt at the film's end.
I wanted to be that prisoner. I didn't think about ejaculation
in those days, though being a hero and defeating my country's
enemies was something that fit nicely into my future plans.

Cellini and the priest and the boy form a sort of scrum
to shoulder their way out of the Colosseum and make their way
home as two of the devils gambol in front of them, skipping
now along the roofs and now on the ground. A month goes by,
and on the last day, Cellini visits Naples and finds Angelica,

who had arrived three days before him, though he soon tires
of her and heads back to Rome. And here am I now
in this piazza, where all is silent, and then the baby cries again.
Where are you, baby? I am not a hero. I never won a war.
But I will help you if I can find you. And then I do:

the baby is right out of a painting by Leonardo or Raphael,
and it stops crying when it sees me, and I don't know
if it's speaking or not, but I can hear its voice,
and when I say, "Who are you, baby?" the baby says,
"I'm you, David. I'm you when you were little,

and I'm you now as you are today," and I say, "Are you
also the David who watched those stupid horror movies?"

and the baby says, "They weren't stupid! They were
readying you for life, for desire and danger." I say,
"Are those the same thing, baby?" and the baby says,

"They might as well be, David. There can be danger
without desire, but there's no desire without danger.
Nothing's worth loving unless it can kill you,"
and I say, "You sure know a lot for a baby,"
and the baby says, "The fox provides for himself,

but God provides for the lion," and I start to say,
what does that even mean, but instead I say, "I loved
those movies. I wanted to grow up, meet girls, travel.
But sitting there in the dark, sometimes I felt as though
I were dying and going to hell, yet I wanted

that, too," and the baby says, "Some call it hell,
some call it paradise. Not the paradise of the Bible,
though," and I say, "What, then?" and the baby says,
"It's another paradise altogether. It's where your life
started, your real life. It's where you began to dream."

Marie Antoinette

It's 1770, and Maria Antonia of Austria says, "Oui!"
to Louis XVI of France and becomes Marie Antoinette,
though it is seven years before their union can be consummated
because a minor and easily correctable malformation
of the king's penis makes intercourse painful. "Ouch!"

says Louis, because, like most men, he gets the whim-whams
at the very thought of a scalpel anywhere near the royal scepter.
Marie is not even twenty as she flip-flops between boredom
and excessive happiness. Why must I be a teenager in love,
she thinks—no, wait, that's Dion and the Belmonts,

two hundred years later and not in France at all but on a Brooklyn
street corner, though the problem is the same.
When you're that age, you're as free as you'll
ever be, also as miserable. "Truth has bounds, Error none,"
says William Blake. When you're older, you have work

and love, if you're lucky, but the teenager has neither
of these, or if work, a fast-food job with lousy pay,
and if love, a love practiced by lovers as clumsy
and inexperienced as themselves, therefore also lousy.
Louis schedules the surgery and postpones it,

schedules and postpones. Schedules and postpones.
Schedules. Postpones. Schedules, and on April 30,
1777, the marriage is consummated. Boy,
do they make up for lost time after that. Unlike a lot
of arranged marriages, theirs is shot through with true love

as well as genuine let's-step-behind-this-rose-bush-
because-I-can't-wait-to-get-to-the-bedroom

button-popping passion. The couple goes on
                    to have four children together, though two die in infancy
and one in prison after the revolution. Each time

we have a quarrel it almost breaks my heart, says Dion.
          In the history museum, teenagers look at Marie's
dresses, her portrait, her husband's portrait,
                    the portraits of their children, three of whom will never be
teenagers themselves. One day I feel so happy, next day

I feel so sad. Some teens listen to their teacher,
          others laugh and goose each other, and some, unnoticed
by the rest, begin to make out, the girls draping
                    their arms over the guys' shoulders, the guys with their hands
on the small of the girls' backs, wanting to go lower

but not quite sure what to do after that and fearful
          that at any moment the teacher will pause in mid-lecture
and call them out for carrying on in public.
                    Carry on, teenagers! Gather ye rosebuds while ye may.
Time didn't wait for the royals, and it won't wait for you.

The days are long, yet each is shorter than the one before.
          A tumbrel has just pulled up in front of your door.
I guess I'll learn to take the good with the bad.
                    A man in a greasy cap bows with exaggerated politeness
as you step into his little cart. A crowd gathers.

I cried a tear for nobody but you. In the dawn light,
          The guillotine's blade shines like an angel's wing.
Vendors sell beer, hot dogs, candy. The people love this!
                    I'll be a lonely one if you should say we're through.
A band plays. The guillotine is waiting. Let it wait.

Man Catches Baby

A dozen women surround me on the museum steps,
    laughing and calling to each other in a language

I can't understand, and then one of them tosses me
    a baby. I'd been looking at Pissarro's *Hoar Frost,*

which baffled critics with its depiction of the shadows
    of trees that are themselves absent from the canvas,

their bafflement based on their assumption that
    the shadows are somehow less real than the trees.

But what is real? When I was a student, my roommate
    Dennis took me out drinking till dawn on my birthday,

and as we walked toward our apartment, we saw
    the guy from the bakery leave a box of pies

in front of a diner. Dennis picked up a cherry pie
    and said, Look, and when I looked, he pushed it

into my face, then peeled a strip of crust off
    my forehead and ate it, and we sat on the curb

and finished that pie and another to boot.
    The next morning, the doorbell rang, and there

stood two men in black suits. One of them
    showed me a card that said FBI on it,

and I thought, all this for a couple of pies?
    But they were looking for someone else.

What is a shadow? Nothing, you say. A lack of light.
    But what if the darkness came first and light interrupted it?

Pissarro's critics were less than thrilled: Jules Castagnary
    saw the absence of the trees as a "grave error,"

and Louis Leroy sneered that the picture consisted
    of "palette-scrapings placed uniformly on a dirty canvas . . .

neither head nor tail, top nor bottom, front nor back."
    Louis Leroy was overthinking it, wasn't he? You have

to see what you're looking at. When I caught the baby,
    the women moved in close, and one put her hand

inside my jacket, but I figured even a bad mother
    wouldn't drop her own child, so, yeah, I tossed it back.

Kissing

Everyone likes it, right? Mafiosi, grandmas, lovers.
Especially lovers. Which brings us to the question,
did Joseph ever kiss Mary? In the Uffizi, you look
at pictures of Mary and Joseph and wonder if he
ever tried to, well, you know. Okay, not that, but didn't
he at least try to kiss her? In Gentile da Fabriano's
painting, Joseph looks too tired to nod to the magi

as they arrive with their knickknacks, much less
offer them a seat, cup of wine, piece of pita bread,
whereas Lorenzo Monaco's Joseph is fit, alert, and not
old at all or at least no older than I, whose days
of producing a photo ID in order to buy a down-market
beer or rum collins are behind him by decades yet
who is as fond of kissing as ever—fonder, really.

What happens in our brains when we kiss? Scientists
say our brains create a chemical cocktail consisting
of dopamine, oxytocin, and serotonin. Dopamine
stimulates the same area of the brain activated by
heroin and cocaine, resulting in euphoria and addictive
behavior, whereas oxytocin, which is released during
childbirth and breastfeeding, fosters feelings of affection

and attachment, and serotonin reaches levels in the brain
when people kiss that look a lot like those of someone
with obsessive compulsive disorder, which is why
the brain scan of a person who's just sitting there
minding his or her business looks like a satellite image
of North Korea at night whereas a scan of the brain
of that same person kissing looks like Times Square

on New Year's Eve. No wonder the memory of
a good kiss can stay with us for years. I mean,
we can't say what love is anyway. Raymond Carver
says, "It ought to make us feel ashamed when we talk
like we know what we're talking about when we talk
about love." But a kiss? That's something else.
That right there is a whole different ball game,

shooting match, kettle of fish. That's the kind of thing
that gets folks sexed up. It's like when Dante sees
Beatrice and says, "Here is a god stronger than I
who is coming to rule over me," even though he never
kisses her at all, and Catherine Earnshaw in *Wuthering
Heights* to say of Edgar Linton, "I love the ground
under his feet, and the air over his head, and everything

he touches and every word he says. I love all his looks,
and all his actions and him entirely and all together,"
even though it turns out that her true love is Heathcliff.
Oh, coulda woulda shoulda. Love is love and not fade away,
says Buddy Holly, also the Rolling Stones. Of course
Joseph kissed Mary. And she kisses him back. Don't they
look happy? And then Jesus is born. It's a miracle.

With You I Am Myself

I am missing you which is probably why I am thinking
of that wonderful Frank O'Hara poem "Having a Coke
with You" as I walk by a French girl who is wearing
a t-shirt that says *Avec toi je suis moi,* or at least I guess
she's French, although why she couldn't be someone
of another nationality who just happens to have a French
t-shirt is hardly out of the question, and, indeed, she could

be someone who doesn't know what her t-shirt says at all,
just the way people get a Chinese tattoo that they think
says *Live life to the fullest* when actually it says *Your mother
is a leprous fruit bat* and that she may have chosen her shirt
simply for its color, which is a charming green, but my
next thought is that, yes, With you I am myself makes
perfectly good sense in that the right person makes you

feel as though you've just been handed a certificate that
authorizes you to be your ideal self, someone who is adorable
and mesmerizing and always bubbling over with life and ideas.
In *The Metamorphoses,* Cadmus kills a serpent that killed
some of his companions but finds out later that the serpent
was sacred to the gods and in his remorse, he becomes
a serpent himself and starts to wind himself around his wife,

gliding between her breasts and licking her face as onlookers
shake with horror, but she, who is named Harmonia, strokes
his neck affectionately and asks the gods to turn her into
a serpent as well, and off they go together, gliding over
the earth but never hurting anyone or fearing them,
"for they both remembered / What once they were,"
Ovid says. Sweet old snakes! Perfectly at home

with each other, with the world. Though there are other ways
to do that: Whitman's friend Fitz-James O'Brien said,

"Why, when I am marching down Broadway, I do not know
whether I am part of the universe or whether the universe is
part of me." And all children feel that way, at least until
they grow up and become us: when you were eight, the world was eight,
and there was no distance between you as you tumbled

around while the the sun rose and fell and rose again,
body and world as alike as two pennies. "Harmonia" means
"well-shaped" or "well put-together," but doesn't it make
you think of music? It makes me think of music. Speaking
of music, a friend who teaches it said that virtuoso violinist
Joshua Bell came to his campus this one time and was practicing
down the hall as he, the friend, was giving a lesson

to a young woman who suddenly stopped and packed up
her instrument, and when her teacher asked her why,
she said, "I'm out of my league," which is when he told her
that the violinist she heard practicing down the hall
was Joshua Bell. Without you, I am always out of my league.
A little farther along on my walk, I am passed by a man
and his son, and the little fellow is wiping the tears

from his face with one hand as his father leads him along
by the other and says, not unkindly, "Do you want to be
a baby or a big boy?" and in this way does the father help
the little fellow to become his best self, to be, in time,
not just a big boy but both the baby who feels the world
as though there is nothing between it and his baby's heart
and the big boy who still has those feelings but manages

to work them into his big-boy need to be responsible
and learn how to tie his shoes and do fractions. Good work,
young gentleman! See? You can be one person one minute
and another a minute later. When I'm the last to board
a plane and make my way through the first-class section
and see all those people reading *The Economist* and drinking
Baileys on the rocks, I think, "Stuck-up snobs!" but when

I get bumped up and it's me who's slurping the free booze,
I look at the people in steerage as they file by and think,
"Scum!" when they're not scum at all and, indeed, should be
pitied rather than scorned because wherever they're going,
you won't be there and that means they will be cheated out
of a marvelous experience which I assure you is not going
to be wasted on me which is why I'm telling you about it

Having a Chat with You

Your friend Loretta reminds me of my friend Allen, who wants to sell
his refrigerator, so he puts it out on the sidewalk with a sign on it that says
"RUNS GOOD," and when a passerby says the sign should say "RUNS
WELL," Allen says that no one would buy a refrigerator with a sign on it
like that. Coleridge says that prose is words in their best order, and poetry
is the best words in the best order. He doesn't say anything about signs
on refrigerators, probably because there were no refrigerators in eighteenth-century
England, although there was refrigeration as long as you were rich enough
to own an ice house, which was not exactly something that could be
wheeled out onto a sidewalk and sold.
                                                  I guess the idea is that if your sign
says "RUNS WELL," that means you're an educated person and therefore
a liar as well as someone who has never kept an appliance in good repair
and doesn't even own a screwdriver. For that matter, how do we ever
communicate anything? Helen Keller had been deaf and blind all her life
when she befriended Martha Graham, visiting her studio often and following
the dancers' movements through the vibrations of the floor, though
one day she surprises the grande dame of modern dance by asking,
"Martha, what is jumping? I don't understand." Touched by this childlike
question, Graham asks a member of her company, Merce Cunningham,
to stand at the barre as she brings her friend up behind him and says,
"Merce, be very careful, I'm putting Helen's hands on your body,"
and she places Helen Keller's hands on Merce Cunningham's waist.
Now when you pick up a poem for the first time, is this not you, your
hands as soft as bird wings on the poem's waist, waiting for it to leap?

T. S. Eliot said, "Genuine poetry can communicate before it is understood."
Have you seen that picture of Marilyn Monroe reading *Ulysses*?
Photographer Eve Arnold said Monroe kept Joyce's novel in her car
and had been reading it for a long time, that she loved the sound of it
and read it aloud to herself to try to make sense of it, though she found it
hard going. REM vocalist Michael Stipe says something similar about
song lyrics, namely, "I doubt very few people in the world can tell you all

the words to 'Tumbling Dice' by the Rolling Stones. It probably holds a lot more meaning to be able to make up your own words and make up your own meanings about what the words are saying."

And sometimes the words are not themselves at all but something else entirely, such as a signal to a bunch of armed civilians huddling in cafés and basements in France to rise up and defeat their German invaders, the creeps: five days before D-Day, the first few lines of Paul Verlaine's "Song of Autumn" were broadcast to alert a French resistance unit called Ventriloquist to start cutting railway lines so the Heil Hitler boys couldn't transport soldiers and materiel to the coast of Normandy.

Les sanglots longs / Des violons / De l'automne, writes Verlaine, *Blessent mon coeur / D'une langueur / Monotone,* which is exactly how I feel when I think of you dying before I do and leaving me alone on this wretched earth, though if I die first, I guess you'll find yourself in the same kettle of fish. Also, whoever's left will have to dispose of all the crap we've accumulated over the years, wheeling it out onto the sidewalk and haggling with strangers over the value of things hardly worth haggling about, though at least we live in the twenty-first century and are thus able to dispose of something like a refrigerator one item at a time; otherwise you'd have to sell your whole house and the ice house with it just to rid yourself of the latter, and who'd want to do that? Surely selling a house then was just as horrible as selling one now. The long sighs / of the violins / of autumn / wound my heart / with their monotonous languor. . . .

When you die and I still want to talk to you, will you hear me? Somebody told me about this inconsolable widow who was accused of blasphemy by the church because the bereaved is supposed to accept death and the eternal life of the dead person calmly, whereas she, the widow, wanted to commission a sculpture of herself screaming and beating on her husband's grave with her fists, and when the churchman who is interviewing her says, "Were you not heard to say to your dying husband, 'If you depart this earth and leave me alone, I shall knock and hammer on your grave'?"

and when she admits that these are indeed her words, says, "Then you pound on the earth in the hope that your husband can hear you?" to which she replies, "No, I pound on the earth precisely for the reason that he cannot."

Everyone in Martha Graham's studio stands mesmerized as Merce Cunningham squats slightly and then leaps into the air, Helen Keller's hands rising with his body, her expression changing gradually from curiosity to joy. Cunningham can feel her fingers moving slightly, as though fluttering, and suddenly Helen Keller cries, "Oh, how wonderful! How like thought! How like the mind it is!" The long sighs of the violins of autumn. . . .

I like that name Ventriloquist, don't you? Since it means an act of stagecraft in which a person changes his or her voice so that it appears to come from someplace else. Where you hear violins, they hear guns—bam! Dynamite. TNT, if they can lay their hands on it. Pencil detonators, grenades . . . ka-blooey! Words are beautiful—I use them—but you have to use them the right way, and now I'm thinking of my favorite street in Florence, Via delle Belle Donne, which means Street of Beautiful Women, which sounds just as good in either language, doesn't it? Sounds exactly the same.

I Wish I Were a Cannibal

because if I were a cannibal I could cook you and put you on a plate
and eat you up but I'd be a magic cannibal so you'd come back tomorrow
and I'd prepare you in a new way and eat you up all over again
or, wait, not a magic cannibal but a cannibal who lives on a magic island
where people who are crazy about each other just keep devouring
the other person every day and then do it again and again and again.
Today I think I'd like to roll you gently in flour, then dip you in
an egg wash and some bread crumbs and slide you into a skillet
in which I have heated butter and olive oil and cook you for three
minutes on one side and two on the other and put a slice of cheese
on you and stick you in the oven just long enough to melt the cheese.
I'd like to make a carrot soufflé out of you. Or a sandwich. But not
just any sandwich: one of those jumbo hot dogs the Chileans call
a *completo* and for good reason because it's slathered in tomato
and pickle and guacamole and mayonnaise and sauerkraut and whatever
else you want to put on it. A *completo* has to have a lot of toppings
or else it's not *completo.* Or a Primanti Bros. sandwich from
the famed Pittsburgh deli of that name that consists of capicola
and provolone topped with french fries and cole slaw and tomato
slices on sourdough. Or wait, I know, the Monte Cristo, which is
truly the Cadillac of sandwiches in that you make it by putting
turkey and ham on Dijon-coated white bread which you coat
with a well-beaten egg and cook until brown on both sides and then
sprinkle with powdered sugar and serve with red currant jelly
alongside for dipping, although you'd be delicious dipped in anything.
I'm certainly not going to turn you into a strawberry pretzel salad!
It's not even a salad, though also delicious. I'd like to smother you,
by which I mean not put a pillow over your face but first make a roux
out of flour and vegetable oil the way they do in Cajun country
and add onion and celery and garlic and chicken broth and then immerse
you and cook you on the lowest heat possible until you emerge tender.
Tender . . . listen to me! How could you possibly be more tender
than you are now! Or sweeter. Notice that I haven't mentioned dessert.

Why would I? You're sweeter than ten desserts—a hundred!
If I eat you and dessert both, I couldn't eat anything for the next three
days except insulin lollipops. I wish you were a shot of whiskey
so I could toss you down my throat or a bottle of beer so I could chug
you on a hot day or a glass of Montepulciano d'Abruzzo so I could
sip you slowly in the presence of one of the yummy dishes I have
described above even though that means I'd be consuming you twice,
which, come to think of it, is not the worst idea I've had lately.
I wish you were a cigar so I could stick one end of you in my mouth
and light the other. I wish I were a cigar as well so we could both
go up in smoke. Let's send smoke signals to everyone on the mainland.
We'll tell all the other lovers to join us. Bring your toques, lovers!
Or should it just be us? Romantic dinner for two or Bruegel-esque
banquet with dogs and children and big thick-bodied Dutch peasant
types larking about to the tune of a drum-and-pipe band? And dice,
of course. Peasants love to gamble. Who doesn't? Why, the first time
I saw you, you were doubling down at the blackjack table, and I myself
am hardly averse to a hand of baccarat or chemin de fer. Did you hear
that? Dinner bell! I think I'll marinate you for two hours or maybe
overnight in umm lemon and ahh garlic and ooh thyme and

Pruno

is an alcoholic beverage made from apples, oranges, fruit
cocktail, candy, ketchup, sugar, milk, and crumbled bread
and whose manufacture, experts say, is "largely confined to"
(I'd say "entirely confined to") prisons and jails, where it can be
made with limited equipment—a plastic bag, hot water, a sock—
and as much time as is available to the guests of the state who

are its manufacturers and who labor under the constant risk
of discovery by those lousy stinking kill-courtesies, the guards.
Pruno is said to taste like a "bile-flavored wine cooler,"
although flavor "is not the primary objective," according to
the Wikipedia article I'm cribbing this part of my poem from
and which does not, in fact, identify the primary objective

of pruno, though I'm guessing that it is to induce drunkenness
in its imbibers, many of whom were probably influenced
by undoubtedly classier forms of alcohol in the commission
of the crimes that landed them in these prisons and jails
in the first place and all of whom took and will again take
the advice of the Charles Baudelaire who said, "You always

have to be drunk" because that's the only way to escape
"the horrible burden of time that breaks your back and bends you
to the earth," and not only that, you have to be "continually
drunk" because otherwise you'll end up "the martyred slave of time."
You want to know who's not the martyred slave of time?
I'll tell you who: William Blake. Blake was four years old

when he saw God at his window and just a few years older
when he walked under a tree filled with angels, their wings
shining. He saw the prophet Ezekiel, he saw angels in a field
with farmers as they made hay, and when his beloved brother
Robert died, Blake saw Robert's spirit rise through the ceiling,
clapping its hands with joy. The Song of Solomon begins,

"Let him kiss me with the kisses of his mouth, for thy love
is better than wine." Thy love is better than pruno, I'm so sure!
But you can get drunk on anything: "wine, poetry, or virtue,"
in Baudelaire's words. And if "in the mournful solitude
of your room you wake again, drunkenness already diminishing
or gone," Baudelaire continues, "ask the wind, the wave,

the star, the bird, the clock, everything that is flying, everything
that is groaning, everything that is rolling, everything that
is singing, everything that is speaking . . . ask what time it is
and wind, wave, star, bird, clock will answer, It is time
to be drunk!" I wouldn't want to be drunk in the mournful
solitude of my room, though. I'd rather be drunk with you.

I searched for you forever! Before I met you, and although
I am not a young woman any more than you are the king
of Israel, I may as well have said, like the young woman
who is the speaker in the Song of Solomon, "I will rise now
and go about the city, and in the streets and in the broad ways
I will seek him whom my soul loveth," and when I find you,

well, look out. And now I feel like fourteen-year-old Judy Hopper
from Alamo, Tennessee, after she was picked randomly from
the crowd at the September 1956 Mississippi-Alabama Fair
concert in Tupelo to meet Elvis and have her picture taken with
him, and when a journalist asked her what she liked about him,
she said, "What do I like about him?" and then "I like all of him."

In addition to being read as a love poem from a young woman
to her king, the Song of Solomon can also be seen as describing
a triangle involving the king, the young woman, and her true love,
a shepherd. Some apologists read it as an allegory depicting
our love for God, but I'm not buying it. "My love is unto me
as a bag of myrrh, that lieth between my breasts." Does that

sound like prayer to you? Sounds like pruno to me.
Sex is big in the Bible. Psychotherapist Esther Perel points out

that infidelity is the only sin that gets two commandments,
one for doing it and one for just thinking about it. Ha, ha!
I love that expression "do it." Everybody knows what
you mean. Nobody thinks "it" means paying your taxes

or washing the dog. Let's do it, shall we? No, let's drink pruno.
No, let's write poems. What's the difference? Let's look
at the sun and see, not "a round disk of fire somewhat like
a Guinea," as Blake says everyone else does, but "an Innumerable
company of the Heavenly host" as he did. Alcohol
makes you see double. Pruno makes you see everything.

Good Seats

Ever wish you had a doppelgänger? Me, too.
Sometimes life just comes whammering at you
every day, and it'd be so much easier if one of you
could shop, cook, clean, and take calls from
telemarketers while the other ate chocolates
and painted or wrote symphonies to rival Beethoven's.
This is called bilocation, which is not for everybody.

Actually, it's not for anybody, unless you're Saint
Isidore the Laborer, who had a reputation
for plowing his master's field even as he was
seen praying at one of the tonier churches
in downtown Madrid. You could also try being
someone else, as did Alex Miller, an itinerant
musician until he was hired to play the King Biscuit

Power Hour show on radio station KFFA in Helena,
Arkansas, which is when the show's sponsor began billing
Miller as Sonny Boy Williamson to capitalize
on the fame of the well-known Chicago musician
of the same name. The birth year of the fake Sonny Boy
is uncertain, since scholars believe he was born
in 1912, whereas he himself claimed the year

was 1899, meaning he was old enough to have used
the name Sonny Boy Williamson before the real
Sonny Boy, who was born in 1914. Now the name
change is understandable—show biz is show biz,
and you do what you gotta do to get ahead. Once you
start changing your birth date, though, you're in big
trouble. Once you begin to think that way, anything

is possible: Kennedy killed Oswald, for example,
instead of the other way around. Actually, I first

encountered the verb "whammer" in James Jones's
memoir of the attack on Pearl Harbor where Jones
says it was a Sunday, so the men had a bonus ration
of milk at breakfast that morning, and "it was not
till the first low-flying fighter came whammering

overhead with his machine guns going that we ran
outside, still clutching our half-pints of milk
to keep them from being stolen." That's also
the last time I ever encountered that seldom-used
verb, yet doesn't life whammer us every day?
Bam-bam—bam-bam-bam! I give up, life.
I'm so little, and you're so big. You're the Greatest

Show on Earth, as P. T. Barnum said. In addition,
you are the earth as well as everything beyond.
And what a great seat I have. Here, you can sit
beside me and watch yourself. Don't mention it:
this is my way of thanking you. It's the least
I can do, also the most. After all, who do you think
I'm writing these poems for? I'm trying to make

you even more wonderful than you are already. That
would sound boastful if I were talking about myself,
but there are millions of us: poets, yes,
but storytellers as well, painters, glassblowers,
cello players, lighting and set designers, actors.
Waiters. Actors who are waiters. Waiters
who never dream of being actors, though you can't

blame someone for turning on the charm if it means
a bigger tip. We all do our part: archers, acrobats,
auto manufacturers, auto mechanics. Bank tellers,
barbers, bar owners. Carpenters, craftsmen, coffee
farmers, and classics professors, just to mention
jobs that begin with the first three letters
of the alphabet and not even all of those. Okay,

settle down. Here we are, front row center,
drink in one hand, hot dog in the other.
The show's starting! Oh, that's right, the show
started long ago. Also, you never settle down.
You surprise me all the time, and not just in bad ways.
Do I surprise you? That hardly seems possible.
But Napoleon surprised you, as did Julius Caesar

and Hitler, also Gandhi, Marie Curie, Nelson Mandela.
Life, you've got a lot more tricks up your sleeve
than we do. Fore! Thank you for those surprises.
And thank you for that half-pint of milk. Okay,
there was a war, but there was going to be
a war anyway; at least there was extra milk.
That was a good thing, that milk.

Forget about that doppelgänger business.
It'd be like bigamy, only worse. Life,
I'd be all mixed up if there were more than one
of me, though it wouldn't bother you. You can
handle anything, even death, which is either
the opposite of you or the extension of you,
depending on which philosophical school

you subscribe to. I know, I know: you subscribe
to them all, since you dreamed them all up
in the first place. Here comes death right now,
as a matter of fact. Hi, death. How's it going?
Can't complain, huh? Yes, I will have
some of your cotton candy.
You're right, these are good seats. Really good.

One Good Turn

I'm actually looking for another street when I turn into
the Via Tornabuoni, named for the Tornabuoni family
and specifically its patriarch, Giovanni, banker and patron
of the arts in Florence, where the street named after him
is located and in which I am now thinking of neither Giovanni

nor his family but of the word "Tornabuoni" itself, which means
"good turn" of the type that Wellesley College professor
Katharine Lee Bates took in 1893 when she and some other
teachers were summering in Colorado and decided to hire
a wagon and go all the way to the top of Pikes Peak, where

she found herself very tired, though "when I saw the view,"
Bates says, "I felt great joy. All the wonder of America
seemed displayed there." When Bates got back
to her hotel room, she wrote the famous opening lines
to "America the Beautiful," which was published two weeks

later and sung to tunes people already knew, notably "Auld
Lang Syne." Another meaning of "good turn"
is to do someone a favor. "I slept and dreamt that life
was joy," says Tagore. "I awoke and saw that life
was service. I acted and behold, service was joy." What does

that mean, though? Service could mean
dishing up meals at the soup kitchen or escorting the blind across busy
intersections, but what is not service as long as it brings
joy to others? One of Naomi Ginsberg's letters to her son
reads, "Get married Allen don't take drugs love, your Mother."

Allen, thanks for not listening to your mom. You did the world
a favor by just being yourself and writing those

great poems. "The best minds of my generation . . .
loned it through the streets of Idaho seeking visionary
indian angels who were visionary indian angels. . . . Dreams!

adorations! illuminations! religions! the whole boatload
of sensitive bullshit! . . . Real holy laughter in the river!
They saw it all." Wait, I'm lost again. Where's
the street I'm looking for? Yet here is the church of Santa Maria Novella
and its Tornabuoni chapel with Ghirlandaio's grand cycle

of frescoes depicting the life of Mary. In one fresco
she's marrying Joseph as the other suitors break their sticks and raise
their hands in anger, and no wonder:
how dishy she is! "She is of an attractive
and ideal height," said Lorenzo de Medici, "the tone

of her skin fresh but not glowing, her demeanor grave
but not proud, sweet, and pleasing, without frivolity or fear."
Then Jesus is born. He's a baby. He doesn't know anything,
yet he knows everything: that we die, that the world
is as beautiful as ever even when we're no longer in it.

Even now you see women as lovely as Mary in the streets
of Florence and babies as wise as Jesus—in any street,
really, in any town. The Tornabuoni Chapel is open every day.
Anybody can walk in and look at these works of heart-stopping beauty.
You don't even have to believe in God, just miracles.

More Soprano, Please, More Tenor

My new favorite Prague ticket taker is the one
to whom I present myself for the Czech Philharmonic
concert which started at 7:30, only I have arrived
at 8:00, since the majority or at least the plurality
of every other musical event I have ever been to
in my entire life has started at that hour, and this is
because he, the ticket taker, says, "The second half

is the best—that's the Dvořák." The first half
was Brahms, about whom the less said, the better.
Well, not really. I like him fine now, though not
as much as I like Dvořák. And even when I thought
I didn't like Brahms, my dislike wasn't so strong
that I didn't have to be reminded of it from time
to time. One Christmas my hardshell Baptist

brother-in-law is visiting with his six-year-old son,
and we are decorating the tree, and one
of the decorations is a tiny St. Peter's Basilica,
and the little boy says, "What's this?" and Barbara
says, "It's a church, a Catholic church,"
and the little boy says, "We hate Catholics,
right, Dad?" Back then, that's the way I felt

about Brahms. Like everybody, I love Bach,
Beethoven, and Mozart, but whenever
I found myself flipping through the program
as I waited for the orchestra to begin and saw
Schubert, Brahms, Mahler, and the like,
I always pointed to Brahms's name and said,
"We hate Brahms, right, Barbara?" and she

would say no, we just don't like him as much as
we do the others. But Brahms was pretty cagey:

when his Piano Concerto No. 1 in D minor, Opus 15 premiered
in 1859, the audience didn't like it
because it had an at-that-time-unfamiliar symphonic
character, and the people in the posh seats were
expecting something they were used to. Twenty-five-year-old

Brahms thought better of his work than they did,
though, so he kept working it into performances
over the next several decades until it became
a standard in the repertoire of concert pianists
and today is one of the most popular piano
concertos of all time. Oh, wait, now he's my hero.
I used to think I didn't like Brahms, but now I do.

In truth, my new favorite Prague ticket taker
is my only Prague ticket taker, since I've been to
that storied city just once and heard the Czech
Philharmonic just once and spent the rest
of my days there wandering the streets and thinking
about music and the lives of the people
who make it and my own life and pausing from time

to time to drink slivovitz and eat sausages,
dumplings, strudel. The more you know,
the more you sympathize: the great love
of Brahms's life was Clara Schumann, whom
he met when he was twenty and she not only
fourteen years older but married to Robert
Schumann as well as the mother of his six children

and pregnant with a seventh—talk about unattainable!
Yet Brahms soldiered on, producing one work
after another and convincing people to love them,
using the method outlined above. Actually, the one
composer for whom my affection has never wavered
in the least is Puccini, and of all his monumental
works—*Turandot, Tosca, Manon Lescaut—*

the most majestic is *La Bohème,* than which there is
no greater tale of woe, as Shakespeare said
of his own great tale of woe, *Romeo and Juliet,*
which itself became an opera by Charles Gounod,
though not a very good one or at least an opera
which music critic Sutherland Edwards called,
following its first London performance in 1867,

"always pleasing, though seldom impressive."
La Bohème is always impressive. Even bad
productions of *La Bohème* are good, though one
in my experience stands head and shoulders
above all others. You know the story: Rodolfo
the writer is freezing to death in his Paris garret
when Mimi, his neighbor, pops in to borrow

matches but faints and is brought back to health
by Rodolfo, who falls in love with her and vice
versa, even though Mimi is dying of tuberculosis.
The usual operatic ups and downs ensue, meaning
Rodolfo and Mimi are parted, though they
are reunited in the final act, at the conclusion of which
Mimi sinks into a happy sleep from which Rodolfo

expects her to awake. She doesn't. Are you
familiar with the expression "not a dry eye
in the house"? That phrase was not coined
expressly for *La Bohème,* but to no opera,
symphony, novel, lyric poem, or epic poem is it
more applicable. And that's just the basic version,
the standard one, the *La Bohème* you'd see

a hundred times were you to attend that many
stagings of Puccini's immortal work. But once
I saw what I might call the one hundred and first

version, a version with not one but two Rodolfos.
How is that possible, you say? It's possible because,
as the curtain rises, the first character you see
is not a starving artist in a Paris garret but an old man,

one who appears to have succeeded in life, given
his lovely clothes and the fine room in which he sits,
but an intensely reflective and downcast old man
who disappears after a few minutes, whereupon
the opera proper begins, though the old fellow
reappears at key moments as Rodolfo and his friends
make merry, the lovers part and reunite, Mimi dies,

and Rodolfo cries out her name as though a spear
has entered his heart. And that's when you realize
that the old man is the wiser, sadder Rodolfo looking
back on the young and happy one and pondering
the follies of his younger days yet their richness
as well, and as your eyes fill and your breath
begins to come more quickly, you can't help thinking

that the old-timer is not just one player in one opera
but is all of us, since we've all loved and lost,
and then you think, that old man is like me,
or if you actually are me, you think that old man
is Johannes Brahms, staggering half aware through
his world and ours as one century puts its head
on the pillow and another wakens. In America,

Geronimo surrenders. Walt Whitman dies, as do
Melville and Frederick Douglass. In Saint Petersburg,
Alexander II is assassinated when a bomb is thrown
into his carriage. Belgium and Italy extend
their empires in Africa. Austria-Hungary forms
an alliance with Germany, and the world turns
its bloody face toward World War I. Vincent

Van Gogh puts down his brush and kills himself
in a wheat field, and Brahms can do nothing
but think of Clara Schumann. "What have you
done to me?" he says in a letter. "Can't you
remove the spell you have cast over me?"
Clara dies in 1896. Brahms writes a final cycle
of piano pieces for her, and in less than a year,

he, too, is dead. Thank you, Giacomo Puccini.
Thank you for teaching me to love Brahms,
for reminding me that we're mortal, that all lives change,
that one lover will say goodbye to the other.
Thank you, artists of every land and time.
Hearts break, you say to us. Love shatters,
you say, and the pieces fly everywhere.

The Woman in the Wall

The housekeeper is about to disappear into the room
next to mine just as I say *Wait, tell me a housekeeping story.*

She's a college kid with a summer job who doesn't care
that she's probably breaking the housekeeper's code

of ethics, so she says, *Sure,* and tells me about the guy
who was doing drugs in 204 last year and got it

into his head that his girlfriend was inside the wall,
so he tore the wall out with his bare hands. Okay,

it was the drugs. But what else was he trying to say?
That the world doesn't work. Sometimes your baby

is right there in your arms, saying *Don't worry,*
we're just going through a rough patch here, we'll be fine,

and sometimes she's in that wall, and you have to
get her out. *We call her the Woman in the Wall,* says

the housekeeper as she laughs and claws the air.
The other housekeepers are older, have taken a child

to the emergency room at three a.m., kicked a husband out,
taken him back. They want the woman to be real.

If she's real, so are they. The driver who takes me
to the airport tells me he'd been a resistance fighter

during his country's war. When I say he's lucky
to have made it out alive, he shakes his head

and waves at the cracked dome light, the grimy seats,
the sandwich wrappers. *Look at me now,* he says.

Legion, for We Are Many

I'm doing a couple of yoga stretches in a quiet corner
of the Atlanta airport because my flight's delayed,
though having said "Atlanta airport," I realize
that I don't have to say "my flight's delayed," when
suddenly a guy I hadn't noticed before says,"You can't do that

here," and I say, "Aw, come on—my back's killing me,"
and he says, "I'm just going on with you—go ahead,"
and he's in jeans but he's sporting a nice shirt
and wire-rim glasses and has a good haircut
and looks fairly smart and as though he's "got some shit with him,"

as they in Louisiana say of people who have some shit
with them, so I put out my hand and say, "My name's
David, but they call me the Kirb," and he says,
"My name's the Devil, but they call me
the Devil," and I say, "There's no such thing as the devil,"

and he says, "Baudelaire says my best trick is to persuade
you I don't exist," and I say, "You don't believe in Baudelaire?"
and he says, "Actually, he's one of the few Frenchmen I do like.
I saw one of those dudes eating a banana
with a knife and fork once, and I wanted to kill him," and I say,

"For real?" and he says, "Ah, I'm just jealous. The French
are okay. Great wine! And that beautiful city.
You know which poet I really like, though? Keats," and he starts reciting
the last part of "La Belle Dame sans
Merci," where the speaker wakes on a cold hillside surrounded

by kings and princes and warriors who've had the blood
sucked out of them by a beautiful vampire,

and as he's reciting, his voice gets lower and lower until he's almost
whispering at the end, which
is when he says "Boo!" and throws up his hands and jumps at me,

and when I start back, he says, "Sorry. I tried that a few
too many times with a girl I used to date," and I say,
"You're single?" and he says, "That's what hell is,
brother. Staring at the wallpaper. Smoking cigarettes.
Watching network television. It does make you want

to fuck things up," and I say, "What about
all the devils and pitchforks and Hieronymus
Bosch special effect-type stuff?" and he says, "Nah, hell's just boring,"
to which there's not a whole lot I can say except,
"What about heaven?" but now that he's more forthcoming,

I'm thinking it's okay to get a little personal, so I say,
"What about heaven, Arch-Fiend?" and he seems to like
this, and he says, "It's different for different folks.
Take the Jewish heaven: Jews don't really believe
in an afterlife, so their heaven's more like a waiting lounge—

not one full of gum wads and dirty diapers like this one,
but, you know. A Crown Club, say, with snacks
and free Wi-Fi," and I say, "Well, what about God?" and he says,
"What about God," and I say, "Is God for real?"
and he says, "Is God for real?" and I say, "Don't be making

fun of me, Prince of This World" and he says, "For the
longest time, they thought I had hypoglycemia. Turns
out it's Tourette's. But as Dr. James Leckman of the Yale University
Medical School says, 'Some people with
Tourette's syndrome . . . sense things in the body movements

of others that the rest of us screen out, some signal
or vibration, some sensory cue. It's almost

like they can see what's going to happen before it happens.'
Now there's a quality that comes in handy
in my chosen profession," and I say, "And that would be . . . ?"

and he says, "I don't know that I could put a name on it.
Read your Bible. Things happen, but they happen slowly.
Forget that 6,000-year shit. 'And when the lamb
had opened the seventh seal, there was silence
in heaven the space of half an hour.' Yeah!"

And I say, "That's good stuff there, Adversary," and he
says, "That's show biz, baby—make 'em weep,
make 'em wail, make 'em wait," and I say, "Speaking of which, I've been
here most of the day, and I'm starting to run
out of gas," and he says, "Hang in there, bud. My best trick might

be to persuade you that you don't exist. And use some
birth control, for God's sake—you people keep breeding
at this rate, in nine hundred years there'll be one hundred men, women,
and children for every square yard of earth.
And televangelists call that a tribulation? I call it an audience,"

and I say, "Now you mentioned God there," and
he says, "Sure. I like different things, though.
Women's basketball. Animal videos. I love the Stones. Whatever
happened to the Stones?" and I say,
"I wouldn't know about that, Power of Darkness,"

and he says, "Aren't you the guy who says art is
the deliberate transformed by the accidental? Well,
I'm the accident. Oh, and I like 'Sweet Home Alabama': it's a better
song than 'Southern Man,' or at least it's the one
that comes closer to charming magic casements opening on the foam

of perilous seas in faery lands forlorn," and I say, "You want
to get a coffee?" and he says, "What do I need coffee for?

I'm the devil, motherfucker!" and starts to get his stuff together, and I say,
"Wait, you never did answer me about God," and he says,
"Oh, I believe in God. I just don't see what's so great about Him,"

and I say, "What about witches—why are they always
so poor?" and he says, "Maybe they're lousy witches. It's too bad:
they're already ugly. Don't get me wrong. Sex is good stuff,
but it can distract you. Nobody ever got distracted
by homework or lawn care, which is why I don't hang around

study halls or feed stores. Give me a bar parking lot
any night. Or a cold hillside," and for a second he looks as though
he's going to jump at me again, but then he says, "Look,
I have to go," and I say, "I got it! You're a producer,
like legendary Bill Graham, only more, you know, devil-y,"

and he says, "Let's just say I'm an organizer. Ever seen
a courtyard filled with people waving torches and pitchforks?
I have," and I say, "What are you working on now?"
and he says, "You'll see: just keep reading the paper.
The Congo's pretty hot. New York's always good for a stopover,"

and like that, he's gone so fast I wonder if he'd even been
here in the first place, so I sit for a while and flip through
some magazines and think about going over
to Concourse A and getting a decent meal at Paschal's,
and the next thing I know, I'm back doing my yoga,

which is when I see a woman I hadn't noticed before,
and she's looking at me as though she doesn't like what I'm doing,
and I'm thinking, New York? Haven't been there in a while,
and now the woman's looking at me
and saying, "You can't do that here," and I think, Aw, come *on*. . . .

What the Parrot Said

My friend tells me his uncle the sailor died
and left him a parrot that nobody else would take
because the bird was so profane, and not long after,
my friend threw a party at his house, and the parrot
was in a cage in the kitchen, and I must have walked
by him a dozen times to get a beer, fetch ice, use
the restroom, and the parrot was silent the whole time,
and finally almost everyone had gone home,
so I went back in to get a broom and help clean up,
and I stopped in the kitchen and looked
at the parrot for a good long minute, and finally
he took a couple of those little childlike steps
parrots take when they're sidling down that bar
they all perch on, and when he got close
to the bars of the cage, he tilted his head and leaned
toward me and said, "Fuck a duck." I wonder
what he meant by that. Okay, he was a bird,
and a duck is another, but why would a duck
appear attractive to a parrot? Another way
to look at it is, why would a parrot think a duck
would appeal to me? That's beyond my understanding
of interspecies romance. Experts say parrots
don't really talk the way we do, that they simply
mimic their owners so they'll be accepted.
But if that's so, why wasn't this parrot more chatty?
No, I think he was just in love with the beauty
of the language: the clipped Anglo-Saxon
monosyllables, the plosive k-sounds of both
the f- and the d-word, the rhyme. Good bird.

Three's Company

As I exit Bed Bath & Beyond with my new three-piece comforter set,
I can't help but think of the French motto "Liberté,
Egalité, Fraternité," certainly an endorsement of everything I agree with
and greatly preferable to Canada's ho-hum "Peace,
Order and Good Government." Sex, drugs, rock 'n' roll. Nasty, brutish,
and short. Friends, Romans, countrymen—why, there are
more tripartite mottoes out there than you can shake a stick at. No less
a figure than Conan himself said the greatest joy
is to crush your enemies, to see them driven before you, and to hear
the lamentations of their women. Why, our own
Declaration of Independence guarantees us the right to "Life, Liberty
and the pursuit of Happiness," though I just noticed
that "pursuit' is spelled with a small "p," suggesting that Life and Liberty
are non-negotiable, whereas Happiness is a lot iffier.
But isn't chasing something as good as getting it? The experts say so.
The signers of the Declaration end by pledging to each other
"our Lives, our Fortunes, and our sacred Honor." It worked!
Thanks, fellows. Don't forget about accidents, though, about
chance, happenstance, contingency: during the American
Revolution, quartering laws allowed the British army to put up
soldiers in American homes, both to save money and so
the soldiers could keep an eye on the comings and goings
of the rebels, but by that time there were sixteen children
in the Revere household, so who'd want to stay with him?
With no snoopy redcoats around, Paul could slip out whenever
he wanted and meet up with the seditious set.
Let us be bloody, bold, and resolute. Let us love all,
trust few, do wrong to none. Duty, honor, and country
above all, though every Tom, Dick, and Harry will tell you
that rum, sodomy, and the lash are as integral
to truth, justice, and the American way as hot dogs, baseball,
and apple pie. Every heart beats true for the red, white, and blue,
but in Belgium your heart would beat for the black, yellow,
and red and in Mali for the green, yellow, and red, and in Ghana

for the red, yellow, and green, though with a black star
in the middle of the yellow stripe. The German flag is black,
red, and gold. *Sieg heil!* Edgar Allan Poe said terror is not
of Germany but of the soul. During World Wars I and II,
a lot of people thought terror was of Germany, but they're our friends
now, and no doubt things will be different the next time.
In that country, "Children, Kitchen, Church" was the nineteenth-century
ideal, though today those words are used derisively
by young women to express their contempt for a social order that,
with its emphasis on brats (children), brats (the tasty
sausage, especially when slathered with mustard and sided with
sauerkraut and German potato salad), and mind-numbing
religious services, is not what those fraüleins would call government
of the people, by the people, and for the people,
notwithstanding the German church's endorsement of the three men
I admire the most, the Father, Son, and Holy Ghost.
Three Dog Night, three blind mice, three-card monte, three on a match.
Two's company, and we all know what three is.
My students think a threesome sounds like fun, but it isn't:
either you'll end up doing all the work or getting
left out or feeling like a hostess throwing a party she's sorry
she's throwing: "Is everybody comfortable?
Everybody having fun?" Let's hear it for the Oxford comma,
which keeps three entities from becoming two,
as when you say *At the party I saw the strippers, Einstein and JFK,*
to which any thinking person would reply *When
did Einstein and JFK become strippers?* Knowledge, Courage,
Integrity are the bywords of J. Edgar Hoover's
Federal Bureau of Investigation. My own university's motto
is Vires, Artes, Mores, which my paymasters
translate as Strength, Skill, and Character, but how would they know,
since no one speaks Latin anymore, even
in Latin America. Location, location, location! The citizens
of every country strive to run faster, jump higher,
be stronger. Let us hold out our hands like a nation of Whitmans
to seize those of the Lorcas, Nerudas,

and Sapphos of every country, state, and municipality. Let us
        build bridges in every way, shape, and form.
A website listing "Countries with the Best National Anthems"
        includes those of Mexico, Brazil, and
the Philippines, though my favorite is the national anthem of India,
        which begins "jana gana mana," which means
"people group mind." Some of the smaller countries use
        the same national anthem music as the bigger ones,
but that's okay, since our own Environmental Protection Agency
        urges us to reduce, reuse, and recycle. And having
begun at the beginning of this poem and muddled through the middle,
        let us now proceed to the end. Actually,
my new favorite national anthem of the last six seconds is not that
        of India but its neighbor Nepal, which includes
the words "Hundreds of flowers, one garland." It's actually 28,980,637
        flowers, according to the latest census, and probably
a good many more during the time it took me to write these lines
        and a hell of a lot more than that in the time
that it took you to read them; still, the basics of education
        are reading, 'riting, and 'rithmetic, and numbers
the size of 28,980,637 or more are 'rithmetic, not poetry.
        Let us pass the thread of unity through
the blossoms of our million selves, no matter how numerous.
        Can I get a hand here? This garland's not
going to weave itself, you know. How about you, reader? I choose you.
        You there, I choose you. I choose you and you and you.

Bernstein's Pizza Pagoda

"A vast armada of supernatural creatures surrounds
the island," says Melisso to Ruggiero in Act III
of Handel's *Alcina,* to which Ruggiero replies,

"Then I'll take up arms," though if you were Ruggiero,
wouldn't you say, "Oh hell, yes!" I would, because
there's only one reason to be alive on this earth,

and that's to fool around with language. All the best
poets do it, including Elizabeth Bishop and Marianne
Moore. On the day of Moore's mother's funeral,

the two friends are riding together in the back of a car
headed to the cemetery. Moore has lived with her
mother for the past four decades and is deeply distraught.

Suddenly, Bishop spots a sign and reads it out loud:
"See the Little Reptile Farm!" Now does that mean
a farm with little reptiles or a little farm with reptiles

or something else entirely, like an armada
of supernatural creatures? Moore perks up instantly,
meets Bishop's eyes, then remembers the occasion

and slumps back. "Maybe on the way home,"
she whispers. Many words mean both a thing
and its opposite: If you eat a cookie and say you're going

to eat *every other cookie,* that means you're eating
the rest of the cookies, unless it means you're going
to eat the first, third, and fifth cookie or maybe

the second, fourth, and sixth. Why does *hold up* mean
both support and impede? If you *continue* something,
that means you will go on with it, unless it means

you'll postpone. If I tell you the Venetians are going
to *fight with* the Saracens, am I saying they'll go to
battle alongside them or struggle against these others?

I just wanted to *toss that out,* that is, offer it for
or remove it from consideration. This is fun: *weather*
means withstand and also deteriorate, just as *oversight*

equals both watchful care and careless mistake,
sanction denotes giving approval to as well as expressing
disapproval of, and *resign* is both quit and resolve

to keep going. For that matter, why does *spicy* mean
not spicy on an American menu and blowtorch-down-
your-throat on a Thai menu? And those are all real words,

not made-up ones like *cacklefruit,* which is what
the Three Stooges called eggs. He couldn't make a snake
out of Play-Doh, say the fine folks of the American South,

couldn't keep a job in a pie factory, has more friends
than a postman with a bagful of welfare checks. Arguing
with him is like trying to cram a wet noodle up

a bobcat's nose. When he lit into me, his voice sounded
like he was dragging it down the side of a cabbage grater.
He took off like a water bug, she's prettier than string

music, he'd slap you down quicker than nothin',
money makes the mare trot. Across the pond, equally
inventive Cockneys say of a friend, "He's me best

China," meaning, "He's me best mate," since
Cockney slang for "mate" is "China plate." Get it? Okay,
how about "I gave him a liner"? Give up? That means

"I blackened his eye" or "I gave him a shiner,"
since slang for "shiner" in that part of the world
is "ocean liner." The most toxic phrase in the English

language is "you always." Say you're in a city
you've never been to before, and you book a tour,
but you're looking at him, and he's looking at you,

and it's been a while, so you say what the hell
and pull your clothes off and hop into bed
and have the best sex you've ever had, ever,

and when it's over, you look at your phone
and say oh my god, we missed the tour! And he says
well you always want to have sex and you say

you always blame me and he says I do not always
blame you, you always say I blame you but I don't,
and you say you always always always! Did you know

that the *Oxford Pocket Dictionary* contains 25,000
words but that 90 percent of the meaning expressed
by those words can be conveyed with only 850

of them? You can do better. And if you're
a poet, you should do a lot better. Christian Bök
says he knows a lot of poets, and they're "the laziest,

stupidest people I know." Ha, ha! For sure, Christian.
I think Christian Bök and I know some of the same poets,
though I doubt that he knows this friend of mine who's

in textiles, and my friend and I are trying to think
of the worst possible name for a restaurant, one you
wouldn't want to eat at even if they were giving the food away,

and my friend probably never took a poetry class
in his life, but when I say, "Pizza Pagoda," he thinks
for a minute and says, "Bernstein's Pizza Pagoda." He wins.

Don't Look

When someone says that, don't you look anyway?
        At the blood, the vomit, the dead man on the sidewalk?
Don't look is like You may not want to hear this

or This may be more than you want to know,
        but what could I possibly not want to know?
Ask of each thing what it is in itself,

says Marcus Aurelius. What is its nature?
        If you can, that is: as Gwen Gordy was writing
"All I Could Do Was Cry" for Etta James,

Etta didn't know that her boyfriend, Harvey Fuqua
        of the Moonglows, was having an affair with Gwen.
And when Billy the Kid sat for a photo in 1880

with Pat Garrett, did he know that Garrett would
        kill him a year later? That was in a darkened room:
Garrett is visiting a friend of the outlaw named

Pete Maxwell when the Kid arrives out of nowhere.
        The men can't see each other, but Garrett recognizes
Billy's voice and shoots him just above the heart.

Maxwell lights a candle, and the two men say yep,
        that's Billy, all right. The body is buried the next day
in the Fort Sumner cemetery, and you can read

the Kid's name on his headstone, although there'll
        always be people who will tell you it's not really him.
Sometimes you can't look. But when you can, look.

The Bad Poetry Reading

It's not your fault that you didn't like it. It's the poems' fault.
And the poet's. The poems were bad, and he shouldn't
have read them. Here's why: every time you give a talk
or teach a class or play a guitar in public or stage a play,
there are always going to be several different kinds of people

in your audience, and if it's a poetry reading, there will be
young people who have never heard poetry read aloud
and are there only because their teacher has made attendance
a course requirement, which makes this your
chance to pull them like fish out of the gray lake they've been

swimming in and release them into a sunlit sea. There'll be
people who've been to hundreds of readings, their eyes in
a fine frenzy rolling from stage to audience, audience
to stage, but also someone who may hear poetry for
the last time tonight, an older person or a young fit one who

is about to have an aneurysm explode like a bomb in her brain
or, most likely of all, someone much like you or me driving home
when the reading's over and coming to a two-way stop,
only the other driver doesn't. Or there's someone who's
troubled, who feels as though life isn't worth living, a man

whose woman has left him or a woman whose child has died:
it seemed okay when it was born, and then it died, and its mother
joined the countless women to whom the same thing
has happened, who knew what had happened yet
couldn't keep from telling themselves that it hadn't,

the way Mary Shelley did when she gave birth to a baby girl,
and after the child dies, Mary writes in her journal, "Dream

that my little baby came to life again—that it had only
been cold & that we rubbed it before the fire & it lived."
Say there's a woman in your audience tonight who

has had that same experience. Are you going to read her
a poem about a shadow that chases another shadow
through an interior monologue, though no one knows
whether the second shadow is the same as the first
or another shadow altogether, and it all takes place

under ice? No, you're not, no more than you'd read a poem
that says man that is born of woman is of few days,
that there's no such thing as death, that the babies are
all in heaven, that their mommies will see them again
some day. Instead, you're going to read something that is,

I don't know, earthy, almost primitive, a poem
that comforts precisely because it's not trying to, one that focuses on
the moment yet glances at everything that surrounds it,
perhaps a funny poem with a dark heart or a sad one that
provokes belly-shaking laughter or a poem that tells a wonderful story

even though it contains chewy little nuggets that are indifferent,
even hostile to story. You're going to write an elemental poem,
one that has three dimensions: you can try for more,
as some people do, but you'll probably end up with none.
And after you've written that poem, you're going to try it

out on somebody, and they're going to like it, because
you have written the poem that has the power to comfort
that grieving mother, console the lonely, give the hopeless
hope. And you can read that poem tonight. Or you can
read a bad poem, or more than one. What will you do?

Lewis and Clark Can't Spell

"Musquetoe," for example. It's "mosquito," Lewis!
That was his name for the wingéd enemy. Clark was
more inventive, with at least twenty variations, including
"mesquetors" as well as "misquitr" and "musquetors."
On the other hand, they were Lewis and Clark:

unlike you or me, who thinks a trip to Designer Shoe
Warehouse with a five-dollar birthday coupon
in hand is a big deal, they traversed the entire western US,
all the way to the Pacific and back, with no idea
of what would happen, whom they would encounter,

when they would return, or if they would return at all.
So to say they are not as excellent as you or me
because they couldn't spell "philanthropy" ("filanthropy")
or "gentle breeze" ("jentle brease") is to inflate
your and my aptitude for cartography, orienteering,

quartermastering, recruitment and retention of personnel,
and procurement of supplies, including but not limited
to longboats, pirogues, muskets, beads and mirrors
for trading, 289 pounds of "Portable Soup" or dried
vegetables to which water would be added, and such

medicines as laudanum, opium, calomel, mercury,
and Dr. Benjamin Rush's laxative capsules, sold under
the name of "Rush's Pills" but known popularly
as "thunderclappers," not to mention quinine and insect
repellent in the event of an attack by "musquetoes,"

"mesquetors," "misquitrs," and "musquetors."
I'd recommend you read their journals for two reasons.

The first is so you, who are no doubt quite good at spelling,
can acquire a sense of superiority so great that
it will buoy you up against whatever discouragements

you are sure to encounter during the period of time for which
that sense of superiority lasts. The second and better
reason is so you can experience the sense of joy
and gratitude the men experience as, for example,
they find themselves sailing upriver through a sea

of feathers three miles long and seventy yards wide
until they reach a sandbar covered with white pelicans
preening themselves as they molt, and later looking up
at the bluffs of the Great Plains under an infinity
of bright blue sky darkened suddenly by flock

after flock of Canada geese, snow geese, swans.
They saw the great mammals—elk, pronghorn,
buffalo—in herds of thousands that forded rivers
in a churning mass, and above them, cliffs two and three
hundred feet high and carved by water over the eons till

they looked like the remains of elegant buildings:
all this and more seen for the first time by white men,
by the two leaders and a sturdy crew, men capable
of "extrodany exeretions," as Lewis wrote, and
"every ready to incounture any fatigue for the premotion

of the enterprise." They didn't know what they were
doing, of course. They didn't know they
represented a government whose policies would
lead to dispossession and genocide. In September
1805, the men are nearly starving, and Clark reports that

the Nez Perce "gave us a Small piece of Buffalow meat,
Some dried Salmon beries & roots in different States."

But a year later, when the explorers tell a band
of Blackfeet warriors they plan to give guns to
another tribe, a fight breaks out; one warrior is stabbed to death

and a second shot through the belly. When they finally
do see the Pacific, Clark writes, "Great joy in camp
we are in view of the Ocian, this great Octean which
we have been So long anxious to See," not even
spelling "ocean" the same way twice in a single sentence.

What have you got to say for yourself, America?
You can't spell, either. You let your Macs and PCs do it
for you. You make me so mad at times, and at other times,
grateful, often in such rapid succession that
I'm both at the same moment. America, you elect idiots

to public office every four years. You always vote them
out and others in, of course, though who can say
if the new officeholders will be better or worse
than the old ones? Keep trying, America.
You'll get better. The winds of history blow toward

progress; they'll steer your ship to the New World.
Oh, that's right—you are the New World. Okay,
okay: at least slavery was abolished, and women
did get the vote, and polio has been all but eradicated,
thanks to Drs. Sabin and Salk. Thank you, scientists!

And you poets, thank you as well. Walt Whitman
loved you, America. America, you're starting
to sound like Allen Ginsberg. Solitude! Filth! Ugliness!
Angelheaded hipsters! Old men weeping
in the parks. America, we're still writing you, every day.

Unspoken

I ask my students to tell a joke at the start of every class
because jokes, like poems, have a hole in the middle,

as in "My neighbor listens to great music. He has no choice."
If you didn't laugh, that's okay. The things at which

we laugh hardest are seldom worth repeating: it's when
they're said, after what, by whom. One student said

he tried to buy camouflage pants but couldn't find any.
Another said he used to think he was indecisive

but now he's not so sure. Legend has it that
when Pygmalion kissed his statue, it sprang to life

and became flesh and blood, but what if the sculptor
had told the statue a joke instead? A word is worth

a thousand pictures, a silence, even more.
George Saunders says he was working in Sumatra

when he was just out of college, and they got their mail
once a month. Someone would go to town and collect it.

He'd been dating a girl in the States, and the first time
he got letters from her, they came in a thick packet.

The first letter said, "I love you so much and I can't wait
to see you again." The second said, "I love you so much."

The Whys

A girl has just pulled herself onto the river bank
    and is trying to explain herself to a couple
  of understandably angry policemen
or, actually, not trying to explain herself so much as say
    I don't know why I did it again
and again as the policemen scold her and ask repeatedly

why she did it, though the girl, not they, is the one
    in the right here, not because she went swimming
  in the river but because there really is no good reason
to have done so and therefore no answer to the question *why?*
    Why is there anything rather
than nothing? For example, why is there turndown service?

Pulling the bedcover back is not exactly one of the Labors
    of Hercules, and as for the chocolate they leave
  on your pillow, it's mid-shelf chocolate at best,
and besides, since chocolate contains not only caffeine but also
    theobromine, which is a vasodilator,
diuretic, and heart stimulant, it'll keep you up all night

and thus counter the intended purpose of the service.
    The driver of the cab I'm taking to the airport tells me
  about his life coaching high school baseball teams
and quelling gang violence in East LA, and when he says his dad
    got married after he'd served ten years
in San Quentin for armed robbery, and I say his mom must have

been quite a gambler to take a chance on a guy who'd
    done hard time, he says, *I don't think she knew.*
  Smart woman, huh? Don't ask, don't tell.
She just took the plunge, and a good thing, too: no ex-con husband,
    no baseball coach son, a lot more dead
Bloods and Crips. Have you ever seen that old black-and-white

movie where the city fellow pauses at the fortune teller's
table to have his fortune read, and the old lady
in the head scarf turns the cards up, and her
eyes get big, and she shouts, *No! No!* and starts to back away?
What does the old lady know that
we don't? When the movie ends, you wait for her name

in the credits, but then the phone rings, and it says
Unknown Caller on your caller ID, and by the time
you get back to your television, the movie's over,
and you don't know the answer or even the question because
you started the movie
in the middle, but then you started your life the same way,

didn't you, you had no idea what was going on
until you were what, five? Six? All you knew
was that the journey of your life was underway,
that you were on the road, and you couldn't see very far ahead,
just to the end of the street,
maybe, but for centuries people have walked from one end

of every country in the world to the other without
seeing any farther than that, though most walks
are a lot shorter, like the walk you took around
your neighborhood last night. Just because it was a short walk
and had no purpose doesn't mean
that it wasn't a good walk. The psychologist Amos Tversky

said before his own early death: *Life is a book.*
The fact that it was a short book doesn't mean
it wasn't a good book. It was a very good book.
The light changes, and my cab moves forward. Back in her tent,
the old lady spreads
a kerchief and puts everything she owns on it, which isn't

much: deck of cards, change of clothes, knife,
apples, a jewel she can sell if she has to.

And then she adds all the whys in the world,
which are numberless yet so tiny that they fit easily,
and she pulls the corners of
the kerchief together, knots the ends around a stick, puts the stick

on her shoulder, and sets out across the world,
taking the world with her when suddenly two policemen
brush her aside as they rush past,
and the old lady thinks of herself when she was young and went swimming
in another river in another country,
and the current was really strong that day, and for a moment

she was pulled under, and in that moment she thought
she would never come up again, yet here she is now
on this bridge, and she sees a drowning girl,
a girl much like her younger self, and she's just about to reach
the other side now, and she looks
again and sees the girl is not drowning, not drowning at all but waving.

Waffle House Index

Snooty British economics journal *The Economist* says, "Waffle House, a breakfast chain from the American South, is better known for reliability than quality."

Yeah, well, fuck you, snooty British economics journal *The Economist.*

Waffle House is awesome, also tasty and cost-efficient, since your meal there will be so filling that you won't have to return to your or any other Waffle House for at least twenty-four hours.

Notice I said "your Waffle House," like "your doctor" or "your church," for just as there are many doctors and many churches, so there are many Waffle Houses, although only one is yours, that is, the closest one, for as every Waffle house is the same, why drive all the way across town to another Waffle House when you can get the same fine food at the one just down the street?

Waffle House food also heals you, just as your doctor does, and it nurtures your spirit, as does your church, and in this way are Waffle Houses even more like these other venerable institutions.

Too, Waffle Houses are uniform in their offerings. Nobody ever drove past a Waffle House and said, "Gee, I wonder what they have there."

For they have everything: cheesesteak omelets, steak and eggs, Texas melts, sandwiches of every kind, and, of course, the eponymous dish that no less an authority than Henry James called an "oblong farinaceous compound, faint yet richly brown, stamped and smoking, not crisp nor brittle but softly absorbent of the syrup dabbed upon it for a finish."

Henry James and his siblings "ate sticky waffles by the hundred," and you can, too, reader, at your friendly neighborhood Waffle House.

And you won't even have to do the dishes, though I suspect the James family had plenty servants on hand for just that sort of thing.

The James family lived in Boston 150 years ago, so no Waffle House for them, because even though there are 2,100 Waffle Houses in 25 states, mainly in the South, the company wasn't founded until 1955.

Life in the South can be difficult and unpredictable. For one thing, we have all those hurricanes, also Billy Powell.

When I was eleven or twelve and Billy maybe sixteen and smoking a cigarette, we walked up to our neighborhood fireworks stand, and Billy talked to the proprietor for a bit, and then he flicked his cigarette into the Roman candle display. The owner cleared his counter like an Olympic high jumper and chased us across the railroad tracks as his entire stand went up like World War III.

Life can be like that in Kentucky or Alabama or anywhere, really.

It can be like that mother-in-law race you see at some of your down-market speedways on Saturday nights, in which the drivers wear paper bags over their heads as they whip around a figure-eight track, getting directions from their front-seat passengers, who are also their mothers-in-law: "Left, you idiot! Left left left! Pull back pull back pull back—not so far! What're you, deaf? I told Kay Lynn not to marry you!"

In this way do driver and passenger alike live out their time in the spotlight like characters in a novel, which genre is defined by ace philosopher Martha Nussbaum in one of her many excellent books as a "complex narrative of human effort in a world full of obstacles."

We become more merciful when we read novels, says Nussbaum.

And when we eat at the Waffle House we become more merciful as well, certainly to ourselves: at the end of each day, the Roman philosopher Seneca reflected on his misdeeds, says Nussbaum, before saying to himself, "This time I pardon you."

And when you order a grilled chicken melt or a Texas steak lover's BLT, is this not an act of self-pardon, reader? And therefore I say order away, for surely those who pardon themselves are more likely to pardon others.

After the food, the best thing about Waffle House is the people.

At Waffle House, you will encounter the same people who were at that club last night. What was its name? I don't remember, either.

There was a 40-watt light bulb hanging from the ceiling, though, and a Circle K's worth of cigarettes smoldering in the ashtrays. A cooler full of 40s. A hotel ice bucket with a jar of maraschino cherries to the side. Drinking glasses for setups with tiny napkins tucked inside.

I think that club was called the Pair o' Dice.

It had a sign that said NO DOPE USE ALLOWED, which everyone ignored. And at the door, an old man you could knock over with a sneeze who had a

Smith and Wesson .38 caliber revolver with a six-inch barrel tucked into his waistband who frisked everybody as they entered.

No, wait, it was called Up Jump the Devil.

Anyway, there was every kind of people there: big ones, fat ones, tall ones, small ones, bikers, queens, tweakers, black ones, white ones, café au lait ones, people who came from nowhere and are heading there again.

This is Walt Whitman's America. So is the Waffle House.

At the Waffle House, the waitresses call everybody "honey."

No less an authority than Harold Bloom said that *Leaves of Grass* is America's "secular scripture."

If *Leaves of Grass* is this country's Bible, then the Waffle House is our church, as previously stated.

Waffle House's scalding hot coffee is our communion wine, and its biscuits are the host.

The biscuits at Bojangle's are actually better, but if you get a sausage, egg, and cheese grits bowl at the Waffle House, you're going to need a biscuit to sop it up.

I guess you could bring a Bojangles biscuit to the Waffle House, but that sounds stupid to me, also blasphemous.

Too, whereas your individual Waffle Houses are known for their chicken biscuits, pork chop platters, and pecan pie, the Waffle House corporation as a whole is renowned for its sound business practices.

In fact, so reliable are Waffle Houses that the Federal Emergency Management Agency or FEMA uses a metric called the Waffle House Index to determine the severity of a storm.

The index has three levels, based on the extent of operations and service at the restaurant following a storm.

GREEN means the restaurant has power and offers a full menu. YELLOW means there is no power, and therefore only a limited menu is offered, and RED says that there has been severe damage and therefore the restaurant is closed.

No sausage, egg, and cheese grits bowl for you! Come back tomorrow, though, we'll probably be open then.

It occurs to me that if you applied the Waffle House Index to America, it would be yellow most of the time.

Certainly America was red in Whitman's day when rivers ran with the blood of men and boys, some still in their teens, boys who would never kiss another boy or a girl or even hold another person's hand, though someone decided they were old enough to die.

Then again, America is green, well, never.

Okay, it was green before the Europeans got there.

In *The Tempest,* you can just see the Old World leaning to the west, its soft shopkeeper's hands shading eyes that strain to pick out the murmuring pines and hemlocks, the empty Eden where life can begin afresh because there are no kings and armies, just a blank slate where Paradise will be inscribed anew.

"O brave new world," says Miranda.

"'Tis new to thee," says Prospero wearily.

At least *The Economist* got the part about Waffle Houses' reliability right.

The Economist does not identify individual writers, the result being that its articles seem to be written by a single author using dry, understated wit and precise language.

The Waffle House menu is never dry or understated, though its language is very precise.

Take those hash browns: you can have them scattered (strewn across the grill to become crisp all over instead of cooked in a steel ring), covered (with melted American cheese), smothered (with onions), chunked (with bits of ham), diced (tomatoes), peppered (jalapeños), capped (grilled mushrooms), topped (chili), or country (smothered in sausage gravy).

Diners can also order their hash browns "all the way," although often you'll hear a customer say, "Aw, to hell with it—all the way."

What does that mean, though? It could mean to hell with snooty British economics journal *The Economist.*

Or it could mean to hell with food snobs—snobs of any kind, really.

On October 23, 2015, globe-trotting gourmand Anthony Bourdain visited a Charleston, SC, Waffle House with local chef Sean Brock, who tells Bourdain he should get a pecan waffle and then demonstrates how to slather a butter-like product over every inch of the waffle before drowning it in syrup.

Suddenly Chef Brock seems to be assailed by doubt—after all, this is Anthony Bourdain he's talking to.

Chef Brock says, "You don't come here expecting The French Laundry," alluding to the Yountville, CA, establishment which has twice been recognized as The Best Restaurant in the World and is famous for, among other dishes, its $85 signature soft-boiled egg appetizer with caviar.

Anthony Bourdain shovels a forkful of waffle into his face and says, "This is better than The French Laundry."

This is the same Anthony Bourdain who once said, "Your body is not a temple. It is an amusement park. Enjoy the ride."

Another notable date in Waffle House history is December 3, 2017.

That's when Alex Bowen, a former army medic from West Columbia, South Carolina, had a craving for Waffle House fare after a night of drinking with friends.

Mr. Bowen entered his local Waffle House at around 3 a.m. but found the sole employee sleeping, so he cooked himself a Texas bacon cheesesteak with extra pickles, ate it, cleaned the grill before he left, and posted pictures of his late-night adventure on Facebook.

A Waffle House spokesperson said that, for safety reasons, customers should never go behind the counter, but added, "Obviously Alex has some cooking skills, and we'd like to talk to him about a job since we may have something for him."

As for the sleeping employee, he was suspended for a week.

McDonald's or Burger King would have fired him on the spot.

Can you imagine what would have happened to him had he worked for *The Economist*?

There should be more Waffle Houses in other states, especially the northern ones, where it is even colder and darker in the winter than it is in Nashville or Texarkana.

At such times you'd think an original Angus cheeseburger or bowl of build-your-own-chili would be welcome, especially if accompanied by endless cups of scalding hot coffee.

Waffle House management should put more Waffle Houses in New York, say, or Ohio.

It'd be like the Civil War, only in reverse.
It'd be a sweet Civil War, a nice one, a war fought with waffles instead of muskets.
The bluebellies would be happy that we've invaded them, and the rebs wouldn't come in second this time.
We wouldn't even keep score!

Oh, Waffle House, how I love you.
How I would love to be worthy of you.
I bequeath myself to the syrup that adorns my waffle.
And you, reader, I love you as well.
The last bacon cheesesteak melt of the day holds back for me, it coaxes me to the vapor and the dusk.
I depart as air.
If you want me again, look for me at the counter, menu in one hand, cup of scalding hot coffee in the other.
Failing to fetch me at first, keep encouraged.
Missing me at one Waffle House, search another.
See? There I am, second stool from the left.
I suggest the all-star breakfast consisting of a waffle, hash browns or grits, two eggs, and bacon, ham, or sausage.
The best thing about the all-star breakfast is that it is delivered in waves: your server brings you three plates one at a time, as if you were royalty.
There, things just got a little greener, didn't they?
Check, please. You can give it to my friend here.
Just kidding. This one's on me.
I stop somewhere, waiting for you.

A NOTE ON SOURCES

Someone who spends as much time writing as I do owes a world of debt. They also owe the world: when students tell me they're tired of writing about themselves, I say it's okay to write about something they heard in another class or read in Wikipedia or on some conspiracy nut's blog. Everything is real: getting stuffed into a locker by a senior when you were in middle school is real, but so is a Beethoven symphony or the fact that Marie Curie won not just a single Nobel Prize but two.

In the arts, the secret to longevity is staying open to everything every minute of every day, which is why a lot of these poems bristle with things I've done but also ones I've read or been told about or looked up. In almost every case here, you can trace a source with a few taps on a keyboard. For example, after reading "Europeans Wrapping Knickknacks," all you have to do is type "Jeni Stepien" into a search engine and hit the enter key, and the first link to come up will be the *New York Times* article from which I took a story too good not to write about.

In a few instances, though, the sources of these poems are less immediately traceable, so allow me to pull the veil aside here. In "Lewis and Clark Can't Spell," most of the facts are taken from Stephen E. Ambrose's *Undaunted Courage: Meriwether Lewis, Thomas Jefferson, and the Opening of the American West,* a real flashlight-under-the-covers book that was recommended to me by a young friend who dropped out of college to pursue a successful career in internet technology but who has, over the years, managed to make himself into a more well-read person than many of the colleagues I pass daily on the sidewalks of my university. That's another reason to stay open. Whitman was right: you might learn more from a barber or blacksmith than from the learn'd astronomer.

A less obvious example of pilfering occurs at the end of "High School." In my description of a fantasy kiss, fans of Henry James will hear the echo of Isabel Archer's one moment of passion in *The Portrait of a Lady,* a scene depicting what one commentator calls "the best kiss in American literary history." This type of petty theft is, again, something that comes up constantly in the classroom. Can you really do that, ask students? In reply, I let T. S. Eliot do my talking for me, he who said, "Immature poets imitate; mature poets steal; bad poets deface what they take, and good poets make it into something better, or at least something different." The emphasis here is mine because scholars sometimes stop with the words "something better" and end that quote prematurely. We're not likely to improve on our betters, but, as I tell students, their work is fair game. Just make it your own.

In addition to literary sources, many of these poems are based on stories others have told me, so many, in fact, that people sometimes tell me a story and say, "Now write a poem about that, Dave." But the best poems come from stories people just tell me with no preamble, as when a colleague from another school said, "This year, last year's Teacher of the Year got fired for having sex with a student." When she thought better of herself, my informant said, "Don't write a poem about that," but it was too late—unless you Mirandize me before you tell your story, it's mine to do with as I please. "Teacher of the Year" appeared in my first LSU Press book, *The House of Blue Light.*

A broader indebtedness takes the form of adapting, not just small bits of language from other writers, but their look and sound, the format of their poems and, to the extent possible, their voice. I always check the lock on the chicken coop when poets say so-and-so influenced their work, because I think the issue is a lot trickier than a simple one-to-one correlation suggests. Recently I heard someone ask a musician who his biggest influence is, and he replied, "The guy standing next to me in the studio that day." Art is the deliberate transformed by the accidental. As much as anything else, it's the haphazard and random that shapes any artist's work. Case in point: I was thinking about how to organize this book when I picked up Diane Seuss's marvelous *Still Life with Two Dead Peacocks and a Girl* and thought, yeah, that's the scheme I want to use, and I did.

Also, for years I wrote mainly what Mark Halliday, in a 2002 essay called "Gabfest" that appeared in *Parnassus,* called ultra-talk poems, ones in which anecdotes, bits of pop culture past and present, and references to books read are woven together "as though the poet is saying, 'These seven or eleven things are swirling in my head, and I feel an emotional circuit among them, and this poem is trying to light up the whole circuit.'" But in 2014, I fell hard for the poems of Jack Gilbert, so hard, in fact, that I began to write so many "Gilberts," as I called them, that I told Barbara that I was afraid I was turning into him. "Just keep it up," Barbara said. "You might start out writing poems like Jack Gilbert's, but they'll turn into Dave Kirby poems."

Then two years ago, I was swept off my feet for the umpteenth time by "Howl" and began knocking out poems that one might call cousins to that canonical work. And just this summer, I rediscovered Frank O'Hara while looking up someone else. So while the pages of this book are dominated by ultra-talk poems, they include as well some Gilberts ("Chasing Jim Taylor," "Sally Go 'Round the Roses," "The Locomotion," "The Woman in the Wall," "Don't Look"), Ginsbergs ("Radioisotope Thermoelectric Generator Ode," "To My Body," "Waffle House Index"), and O'Haras ("With You I Am Myself," "Having a Chat with You"). Who's next, I wonder.

Should the settings of some of these poems suggest that my travel budget is greater than it is, let me express here my gratitude to Florida State University's International Programs office, which has sent me to teach in Italy eight times, and to Mark Pietralunga and Karen Myers for opening my eyes to that country's hidden treasures.

My greatest debt always is to Barbara Hamby, award-winning poet and fiction writer, cherished colleague, tireless traveling companion. When I met Barbara, I stepped through a door and found myself in a life newer, richer, and freer than any I'd known before. I've never looked back.